# English PUZZLES

## 4

## DOUG CASE

HEINEMANN

# Heinemann Games Series

**Titles in this series include:**

| | | |
|---|---|---|
| **English Puzzles 1** | Doug Case | 0 435 28280 8 |
| **English Puzzles 2** | Doug Case | 0 435 28281 6 |
| **English Puzzles 3** | Doug Case | 0 435 28282 4 |
| **English Puzzles 4** | Doug Case | 0 435 28283 2 |

**Play Games With English Book 1**   Colin Granger   0 435 28060 0
Teacher's Book 1   0 435 28061 9
**Play Games With English Book 2**   Colin Granger   0 435 28062 7
Teacher's Book 2   0 435 28063 5

**Word Games with English 1**   Deirdre Howard-Williams & Cynthia Herd   0 435 28380 4
**Word Games with English 2**   Deirdre Howard-Williams & Cynthia Herd   0 435 28381 2
**Word Games with English 3**   Deirdre Howard-Williams & Cynthia Herd   0 435 28382 0
**Word Games with English Plus**   Deirdre Howard-Williams & Cynthia Herd   0 435 28379 0

ALBSU RESOURCE CENTRE
at the INSTITUTE OF EDUCATION
UNIVERSITY OF LONDON
LIBRARY
20 BEDFORD WAY,
LONDON, WC1H 0AL

17 MAY 1995

Heinemann International
a division of Heinemann Publishers (Oxford) Ltd.,
Halley Court, Jordan Hill, Oxford OX2 8EJ

OXFORD   LONDON   EDINBURGH   MADRID   PARIS   ATHENS   BOLOGNA
MELBOURNE   SYDNEY   AUCKLAND   IBADAN   NAIROBI   GABORONE   HARARE
PORTSMOUTH (NH)   SINGAPORE   TOKYO

ISBN 0 435 28283 2

© Doug Case 1991
First Published 1991

All rights reserved; no part of this publication may be reproduced, stored in a retrieval system, or transmitted in any form or by any means, electronic, mechanical, photocopying, recording or otherwise, without the prior written permission of the Publishers.

**Acknowledgements**

Thanks to Brigitte Zacharian for help in testing the puzzles in this book, to Michèle Cronick and Charlotte Covill for deft and thoughtful editing, and to them all for many valuable suggestions.

Illustrated by Nick Duffy, Belinda Evans, John Lobban and Laura Potter
Designed and typeset by Plum Design, Southampton
Printed by Thomson Litho Ltd, East Kilbride, Scotland

93  94  95  96     10  9  8  7  6  5  4  3

# Contents

| | | | | |
|---|---|---|---|---|
| **Introduction** | | | pages | iv-vi |
| **Puzzles** | | | pages | 1-50 |

| | | | | |
|---|---|---|---|---|
| 1 | Be careful! | 26 | The second half |
| 2 | Geography and geometry | 27 | Grammatical terms |
| 3 | Twenty-one proverbs | 28 | Shopping list |
| 4 | Bus queue | 29 | More logical laws |
| 5 | Find the key word | 30 | A very *polite* jigsaw |
| 6 | Missing letters | 31 | Titles and authors |
| 7 | Science fiction | 32 | Typing mistakes |
| 8 | Exclamations! | 33 | The World Cup |
| 9 | Imaginary jobs and real jobs | 34 | Hotel rooms |
| 10 | Pairs of words | 35 | Bricks in a wall |
| 11 | Abbreviations | 36 | A phonetic crossword |
| 12 | A strange quiz | 37 | Knock! Knock! |
| 13 | A very *official* jigsaw | 38 | On the telephone |
| 14 | Grammar files | 39 | Eight special days |
| 15 | Documents for the files | 40 | Dictionary definitions |
| 16 | Strong feelings | 41 | Punctuation |
| 17 | Telegram language | 42 | Folded twice |
| 18 | Logical laws | 43 | Close the shutters |
| 19 | At the theatre | 44 | A colloquial crossword |
| 20 | Disc jockey | 45 | Double meanings |
| 21 | House and garden | 46 | A very *emphatic* jigsaw |
| 22 | What do they *really* mean? | 47 | Misprints |
| 23 | Interesting facts | 48 | Bits and pieces |
| 24 | Folded paper | 49 | Contractions |
| 25 | What are they saying? | 50 | The last word |

| | | | |
|---|---|---|---|
| **Solutions** | | pages | 51-57 |
| **Index** | | page | 58 |

# Introduction

There are fifty puzzles in this book. They all help you to practise your English. This Introduction gives you some useful words. You often find these words in the instructions for English puzzles. (If you know Book 1, Book 2 or Book 3 in this series, you already know most of these words.)

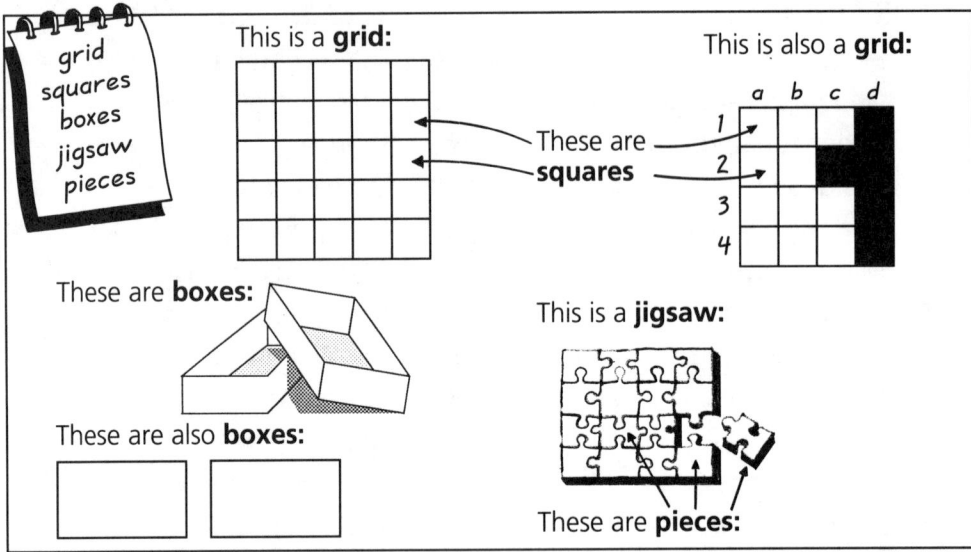

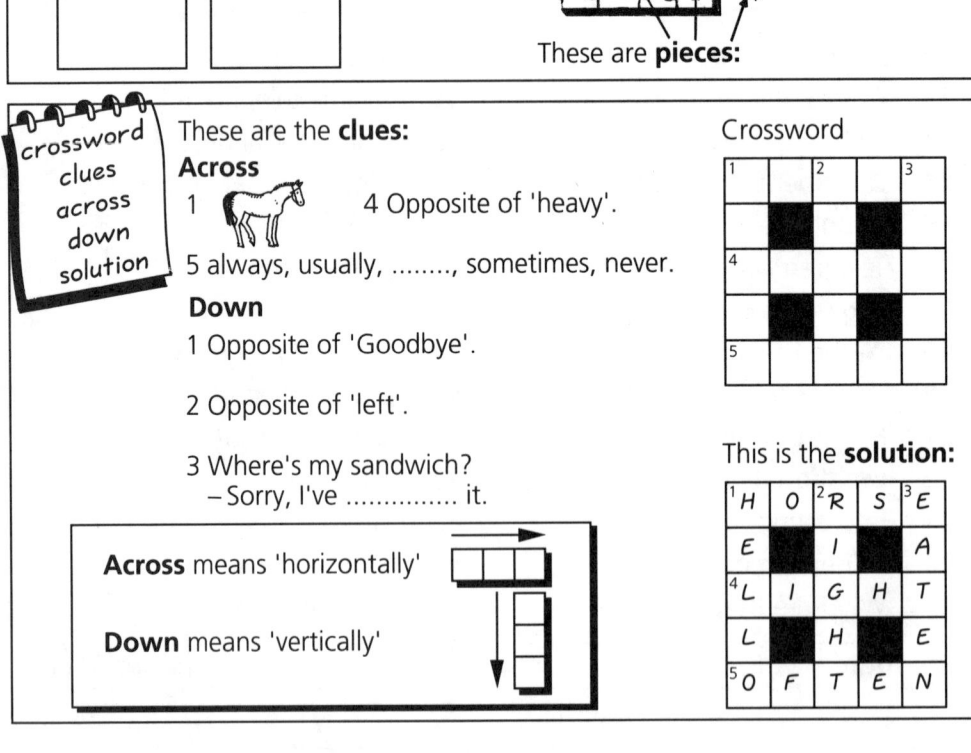

*grid*
*squares*
*boxes*
*jigsaw*
*pieces*

This is a **grid**:

This is also a **grid**:

These are **squares**

These are **boxes**:

These are also **boxes**:

This is a **jigsaw**:

These are **pieces**:

*crossword*
*clues*
*across*
*down*
*solution*

These are the **clues**:

**Across**
1 🐎
4 Opposite of 'heavy'.
5 always, usually, ........, sometimes, never.

**Down**
1 Opposite of 'Goodbye'.
2 Opposite of 'left'.
3 Where's my sandwich?
   – Sorry, I've ............... it.

Crossword

This is the **solution**:

| ¹H | O | ²R | S | ³E |
|---|---|---|---|---|
| E |   | I |   | A |
| ⁴L | I | G | H | T |
| L |   | H |   | E |
| ⁵O | F | T | E | N |

**Across** means 'horizontally'

**Down** means 'vertically'

iv

line
list
pair
group
spaces

This is a **line** of words:

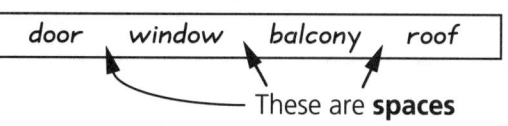

| door | window | balcony | roof |

These are **spaces**

This is a **list** of names:

Elvis Presley
Phil Collins
Tina Turner
Mick Jagger
Annie Lennox

This is a **pair** of symbols:

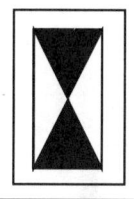

This is a **group** of pictures:

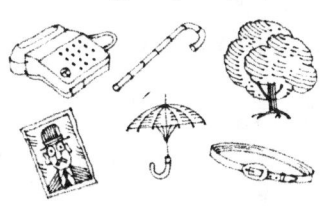

---

complete
missing
the wrong order
the right order
spelling mistake
riddle

This word is not **complete**. Two letters are **missing:**

W ND W

(The missing letters are I and O. The complete word is WINDOW.)

In this word, the letters are in **the wrong order:**

ODRO

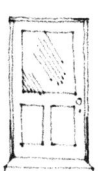

(**The right order** – or the correct order – is DOOR.)

In this word, there is a **spelling mistake:**

BALCENY

(The correct spelling is BALCONY.)

This is a **riddle** (a question which seems difficult to answer):

WHAT GOES THROUGH A DOOR, BUT NEVER GOES IN AND NEVER COMES OUT?

(The answer is: A keyhole.)

v

add
complete
correct
fill in
label

**Add** a letter:

C A N → ☐ ☐ ☐ ☐   C A N E

**Complete** this film title:

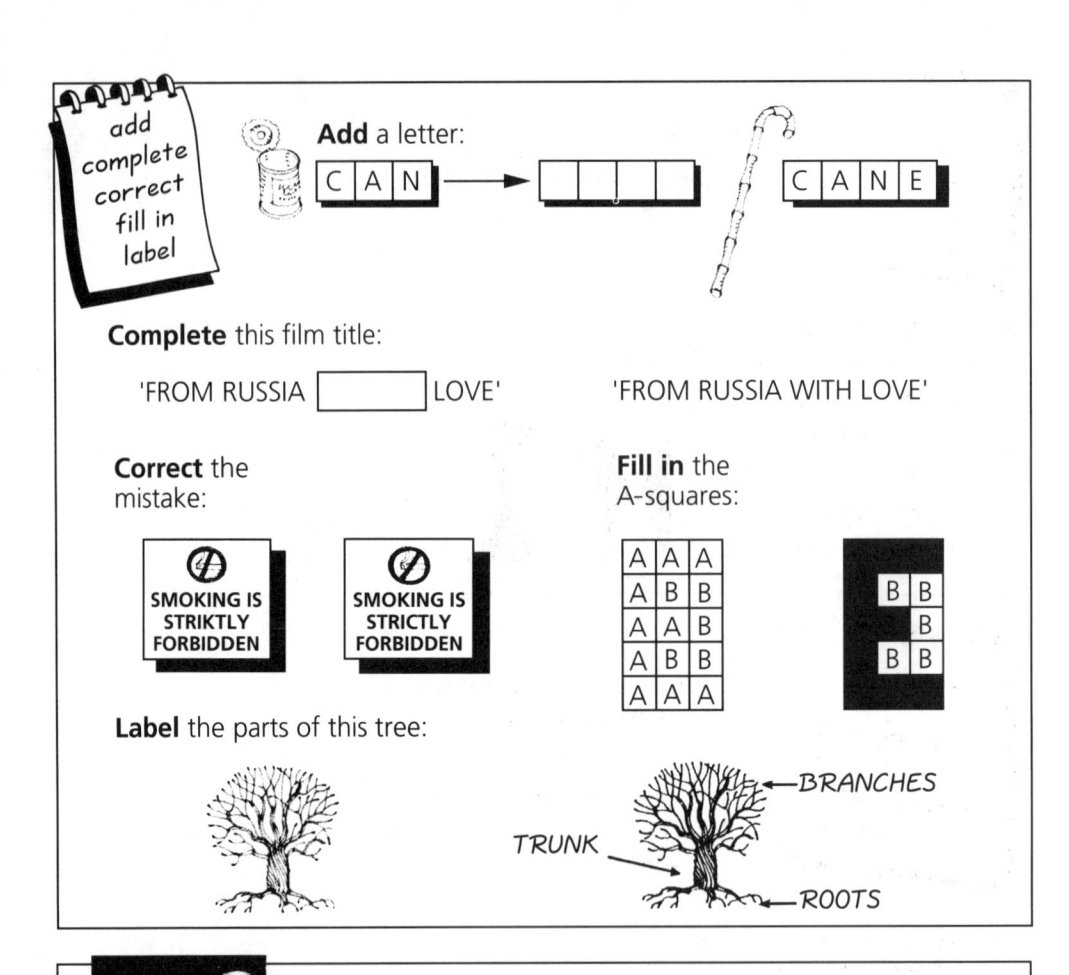

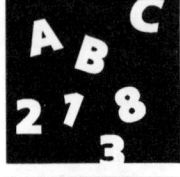

'FROM RUSSIA ☐ LOVE'   'FROM RUSSIA WITH LOVE'

**Correct** the mistake:

SMOKING IS STRIKTLY FORBIDDEN   SMOKING IS STRICTLY FORBIDDEN

**Fill in** the A-squares:

| A | A | A |
| A | B | B |
| A | A | B |
| A | B | B |
| A | A | A |

**Label** the parts of this tree:

←BRANCHES
TRUNK
←ROOTS

Enjoy doing the puzzles – and remember: when there are letters or numbers in a puzzle, say them to yourself in *English*.

Use a *pencil*, in case you make a mistake!

You can find the *solutions* at the back of the book.

# BE CAREFUL ⚠

Write the correct warning in each picture. All the words you need are in the grid.

| NO | OFF | PAINT | IS | SWIMMING | OF |
|---|---|---|---|---|---|
| CAN | VEHICLE | REDUCE | THE | DAMAGE | KEEP |
| HEALTH | STEP | WHEN | MIND | FLAG | NOW |
| BEWARE | SERIOUSLY | DOG | GRASS | WET | PICKPOCKETS |
| THE | DANGER | BEWARE | LONG | CIGARETTES | THE |
| FLYING | SPEED | THE | YOUR | OF | RED |

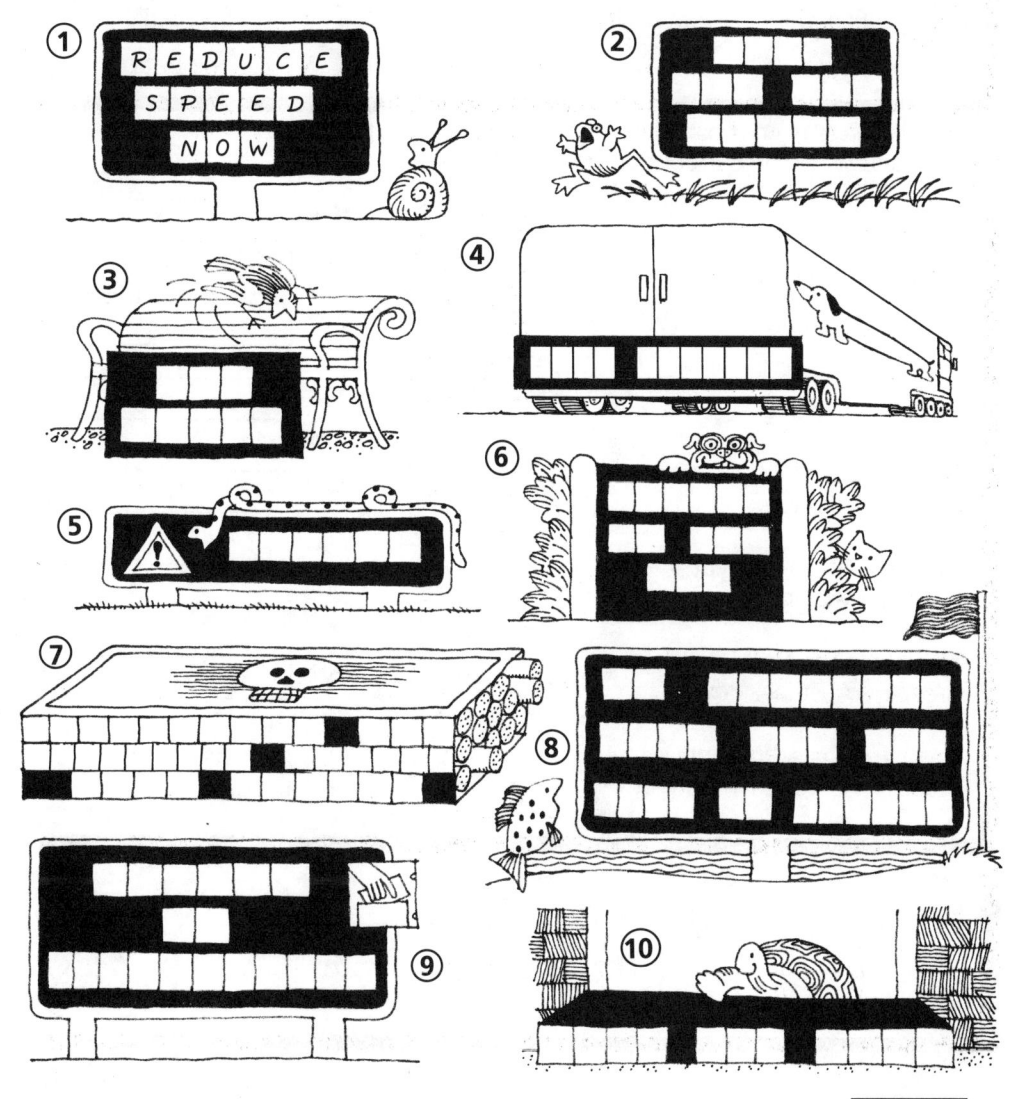

① REDUCE SPEED NOW

English Puzzles 4    Heinemann International

PUZZLE 1

# Geography and geometry

If you see a *GB* plate on a car, you know the car comes from Great Britain.
Here are the plates which identify eighteen other countries:

| | | | | | |
|---|---|---|---|---|---|
| A | Austria | GR | Greece | N | Norway |
| DY | Benin | RH | Haiti | PE | Peru |
| CO | Colombia | IRL | Ireland | R | Romania |
| C | Cuba | IL | Israel | E | Spain |
| EC | Ecuador | LAO | Laos | S | Sweden |
| ET | Egypt | NL | The Netherlands | V | The Vatican City |

Using the letters from those plates, find the words for the shapes in the box below – and write the correct number in each shape.

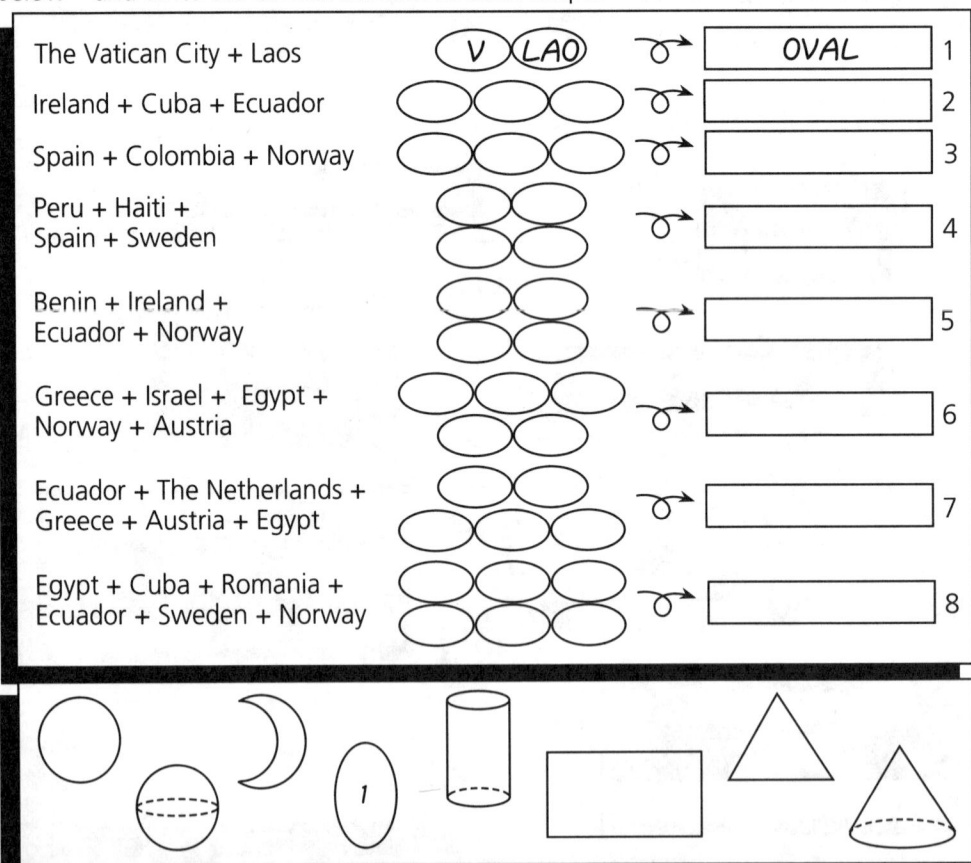

| | | | |
|---|---|---|---|
| The Vatican City + Laos | V LAO | → | OVAL | 1 |
| Ireland + Cuba + Ecuador | | → | | 2 |
| Spain + Colombia + Norway | | → | | 3 |
| Peru + Haiti + Spain + Sweden | | → | | 4 |
| Benin + Ireland + Ecuador + Norway | | → | | 5 |
| Greece + Israel + Egypt + Norway + Austria | | → | | 6 |
| Ecuador + The Netherlands + Greece + Austria + Egypt | | → | | 7 |
| Egypt + Cuba + Romania + Ecuador + Sweden + Norway | | → | | 8 |

**PUZZLE** 2          English Puzzles 4   Heinemann International

# Twenty-one proverbs

In the grid, there are twenty-one English proverbs. Three are already complete: Number 7, *Don't cry before you're hurt*, Number 12, *Time flies*, and Number 19, *Money talks*. Complete the others.

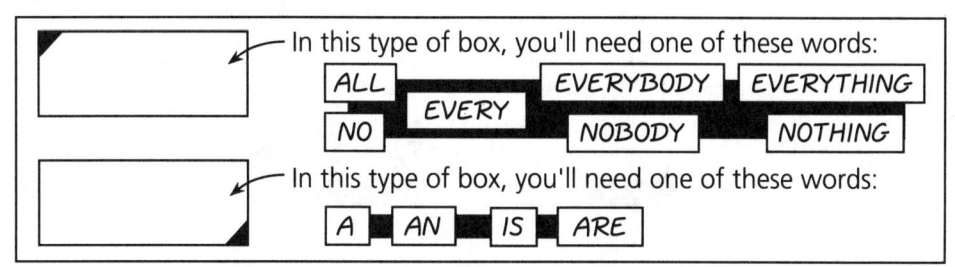

In this type of box, you'll need one of these words:
ALL — EVERYBODY — EVERYTHING — NO — EVERY — NOBODY — NOTHING

In this type of box, you'll need one of these words:
A — AN — IS — ARE

| 1 EVERY-THING | MUST | HAVE | | BEGIN-NING | 2 SOME-THING | | BETTER | THAN | 3 |
|---|---|---|---|---|---|---|---|---|---|
| | | 5 | | | | | | | |
| 4 ASK | | QUES-TIONS | AND | YOU'LL | HEAR | | LIES | | CERTAIN |
| | NEWS | | | 8 | | | | | EXCEPT |
| 6 SEEING | | BELIEV-ING | 7 DON'T | CRY | BEFORE | YOU'RE | HURT | | DEATH |
| | GOOD | | PUT | | | | | | AND |
| 9 | NEWS | | 10 | ROADS | LEAD | TO | ROME | | TAXES |
| LOVE | | 11 | YOUR | | | | 12 | | 13 |
| MAKES | | THERE | EGGS | | | | TIME | | |
| 14 | CATS | | GREY | IN | THE | DARK | FLIES | | FRIEND |
| HARD | | TWO | ONE | | | | | | TO |
| HEARTS | | SIDES | BASKET | | 15 YOU | CAN'T | PLEASE | | |
| GENTLE | | TO | | | | | | | |
| | 16 | PICTURE | TELLS | | STORY | 17 | | | |
| | 18 | QUES-TION | | | | 19 MONEY | TALKS | | FRIEND |
| | IT'S | | | | | ISN'T | | | TO |
| 20 THERE'S | | TIME | AND | | PLACE | FOR | | | |
| | SMALL | | | | | | | | |
| | WORLD | 21 | | GOOD | THINGS | MUST | COME | TO | END |

Question: Are any of those proverbs similar to proverbs in your language?

English Puzzles 4    Heinemann International    **PUZZLE 3**

# BUS QUEUE

Look at this question: **Working hard?** The *complete* question would be 'Are you working hard?' In informal speech, it's possible to omit words like *Are you*, *Do you* and *Have you* from the beginning of a question.

Look at the picture below. Read what the people in the bus queue are saying, and decide which words they have omitted: ARE YOU / DO YOU / DID YOU / WOULD YOU / HAVE YOU

Write the complete questions in the boxes.

- Been waiting long?
- Think it's going to rain?
- Like a piece of chocolate?
- Tired?
- Lost something?
- See the match on TV last night?
- Seen any good films lately?
- Having a holiday this year?
- Need any help?

PUZZLE 4        English Puzzles 4    Heinemann International

# Find the key word

## JUKEBOX

A word is missing from the title of each song on the jukebox – *the same word* in all the titles. Decide what this 'key word' is, and then do the second part of the puzzle.

| 1<br>___ your life<br>THE AVERAGE WHITE BAND | 6<br>I ___ to listen to Beethoven<br>THE EURYTHMICS | 11<br>You know I ___ you, don't you?<br>HOWARD JONES | 16<br>___ me<br>DIANA ROSS |
|---|---|---|---|
| 2<br>Goodbye to ___<br>THE CARPENTERS | 7<br>You always hurt the one you ___<br>CONNIE FRANCIS | 12<br>You gave me somebody to ___<br>MANFRED MANN | 17<br>___ the one you're with<br>STEPHEN STILLS |
| 3<br>You made me ___ you<br>NAT KING COLE | 8<br>The power of ___<br>FRANKIE GOES TO HOLLYWOOD | 13<br>You don't have to say you ___ me<br>ELVIS PRESLEY | 18<br>To know him is to ___ him<br>THE TEDDY BEARS |
| 4<br>The meaning of ___<br>DEPECHE MODE | 9<br>___ or money<br>SAMMY HAGAR | 14<br>This is not a ___ song<br>PUBLIC IMAGE LTD | 19<br>Still in ___ with you<br>THIN LIZZY |
| 5<br>I've just begun to ___ you<br>DYNASTY | 10<br>I ___ rock'n'roll<br>JOAN JETT | 15<br>We ___ you<br>THE ROLLING STONES | 20<br>In the name of ___<br>U2 |

In some of the titles, the 'key word' is a *noun*; in others, it is a *verb* (in the *infinitive*, the *imperative* or the *Present Simple*). Write the numbers of the songs here:

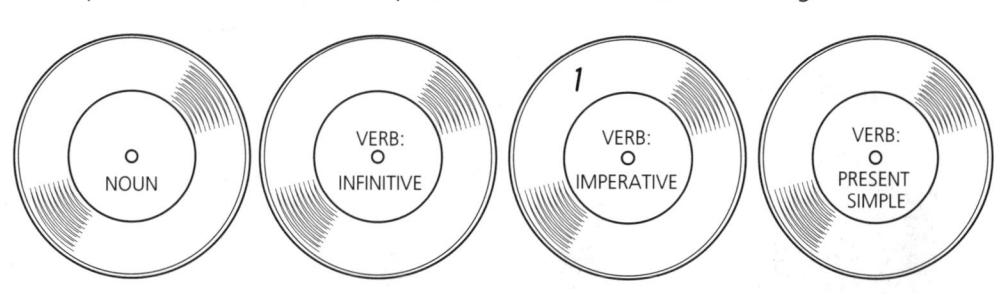

- NOUN
- VERB: INFINITIVE
- VERB: IMPERATIVE — 1
- VERB: PRESENT SIMPLE

English Puzzles 4   Heinemann International

PUZZLE 5

# Missing letters

First, complete the ten words in the grid by putting in the missing letters.
Here's a little help:
– All the words are Past Participles.
– The *last* letter of each word is the same.
– All the *other* missing letters are vowels (A,E,I,O,U).

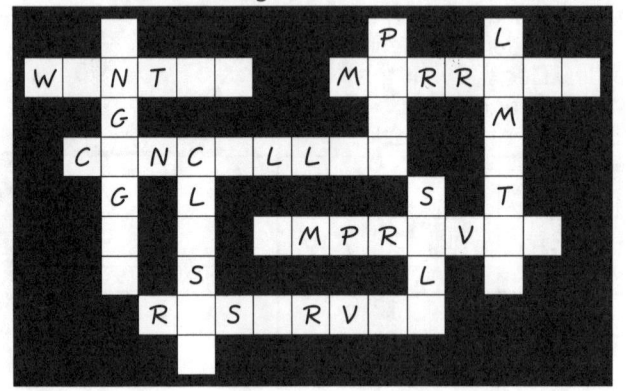

Put one of the completed words from the grid into each of the pictures.

PUZZLE 6                English Puzzles 4    Heinemann International

# Science fiction

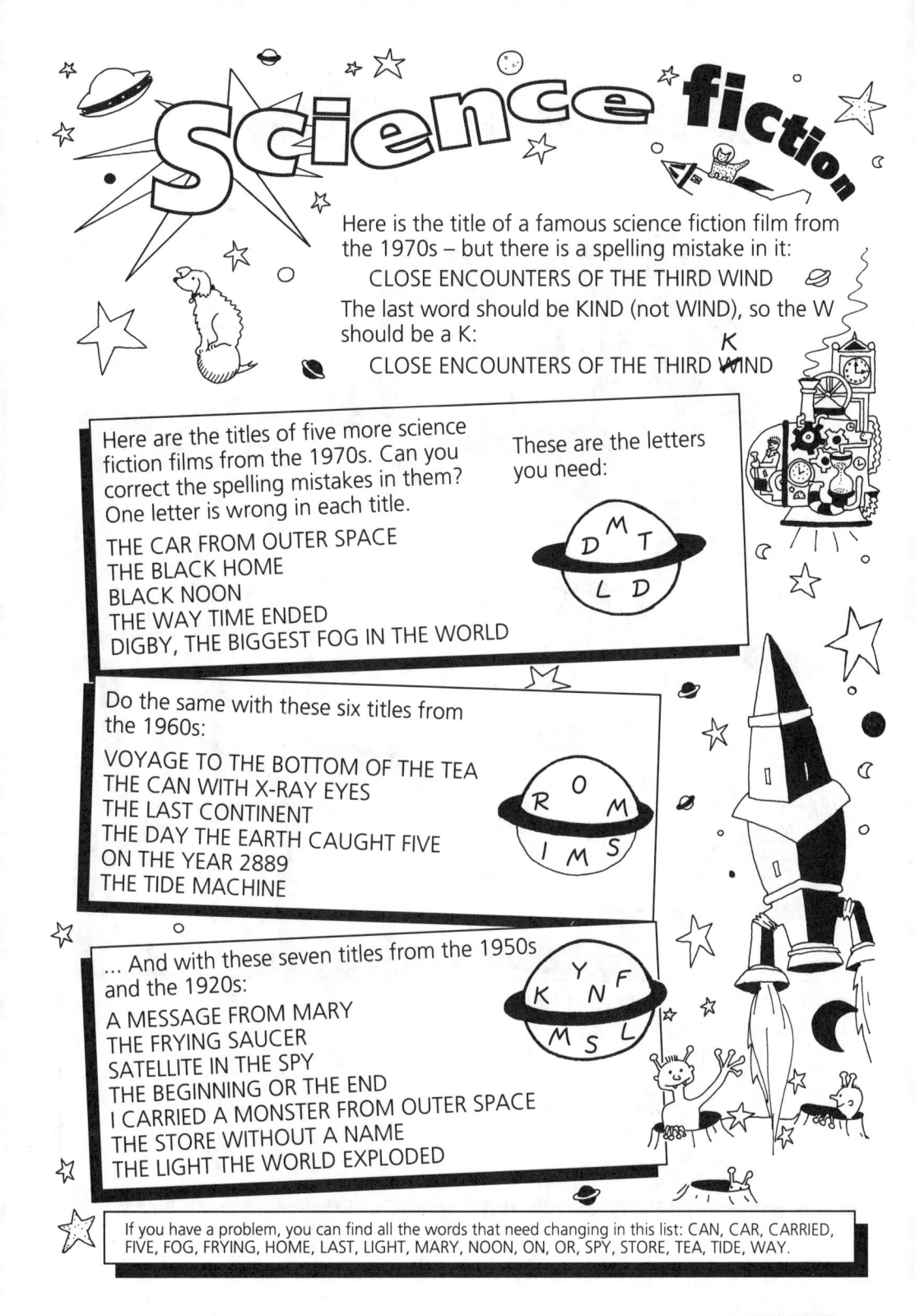

Here is the title of a famous science fiction film from the 1970s – but there is a spelling mistake in it:

CLOSE ENCOUNTERS OF THE THIRD WIND

The last word should be KIND (not WIND), so the W should be a K:

CLOSE ENCOUNTERS OF THE THIRD W̶IND  K

Here are the titles of five more science fiction films from the 1970s. Can you correct the spelling mistakes in them? One letter is wrong in each title.

THE CAR FROM OUTER SPACE
THE BLACK HOME
BLACK NOON
THE WAY TIME ENDED
DIGBY, THE BIGGEST FOG IN THE WORLD

These are the letters you need: D M T L D

Do the same with these six titles from the 1960s:

VOYAGE TO THE BOTTOM OF THE TEA
THE CAN WITH X-RAY EYES
THE LAST CONTINENT
THE DAY THE EARTH CAUGHT FIVE
ON THE YEAR 2889
THE TIDE MACHINE

R O M I M S

... And with these seven titles from the 1950s and the 1920s:

A MESSAGE FROM MARY
THE FRYING SAUCER
SATELLITE IN THE SPY
THE BEGINNING OR THE END
I CARRIED A MONSTER FROM OUTER SPACE
THE STORE WITHOUT A NAME
THE LIGHT THE WORLD EXPLODED

K Y N F M S L

If you have a problem, you can find all the words that need changing in this list: CAN, CAR, CARRIED, FIVE, FOG, FRYING, HOME, LAST, LIGHT, MARY, NOON, ON, OR, SPY, STORE, TEA, TIDE, WAY.

English Puzzles 4    Heinemann International

PUZZLE 7

# Exclamations!

There are eleven English exclamations in the grid. Put the correct one into each of the pictures.

```
      H E Y !
      A         W
B R R !   O U C H !
      H     G   O
    W A T C H O O !
  B O O !   !   P
    W           S H H !
    !     M M M !
```

Put one of the exclamations before each of these sentences.
(Use each exclamation once.)

_____! I'm freezing!                 _____! I think I'm getting a cold.
_____! That hurt!                    _____! This is delicious!
_____! Rubbish!                      _____! This tastes awful!
_____! Come back!                    _____! Oh dear, it's broken.
_____! Very funny.                   _____! That's fantastic!
_____! The baby's asleep.

Question: Can you *pronounce* all those exclamations?

PUZZLE 8                              English Puzzles 4    Heinemann International

# Imaginary jobs and real jobs

Here are two imaginary jobs:

**window operator**

**telephone cleaner**

And here are two real jobs:

**window cleaner**

**telephone operator**

From this list of twelve imaginary jobs, put the correct first and second parts together to find the real jobs shown in the pictures. Write each real job under the correct picture.

| | |
|---|---|
| computer | dancer |
| hotel | photographer |
| driving | manager |
| newspaper | singer |
| opera | programmer |
| rock | worker |
| film | driver |
| aircraft | director |
| ballet | editor |
| construction | instructor |
| lorry | musician |
| wedding | technician |

English Puzzles 4   Heinemann International

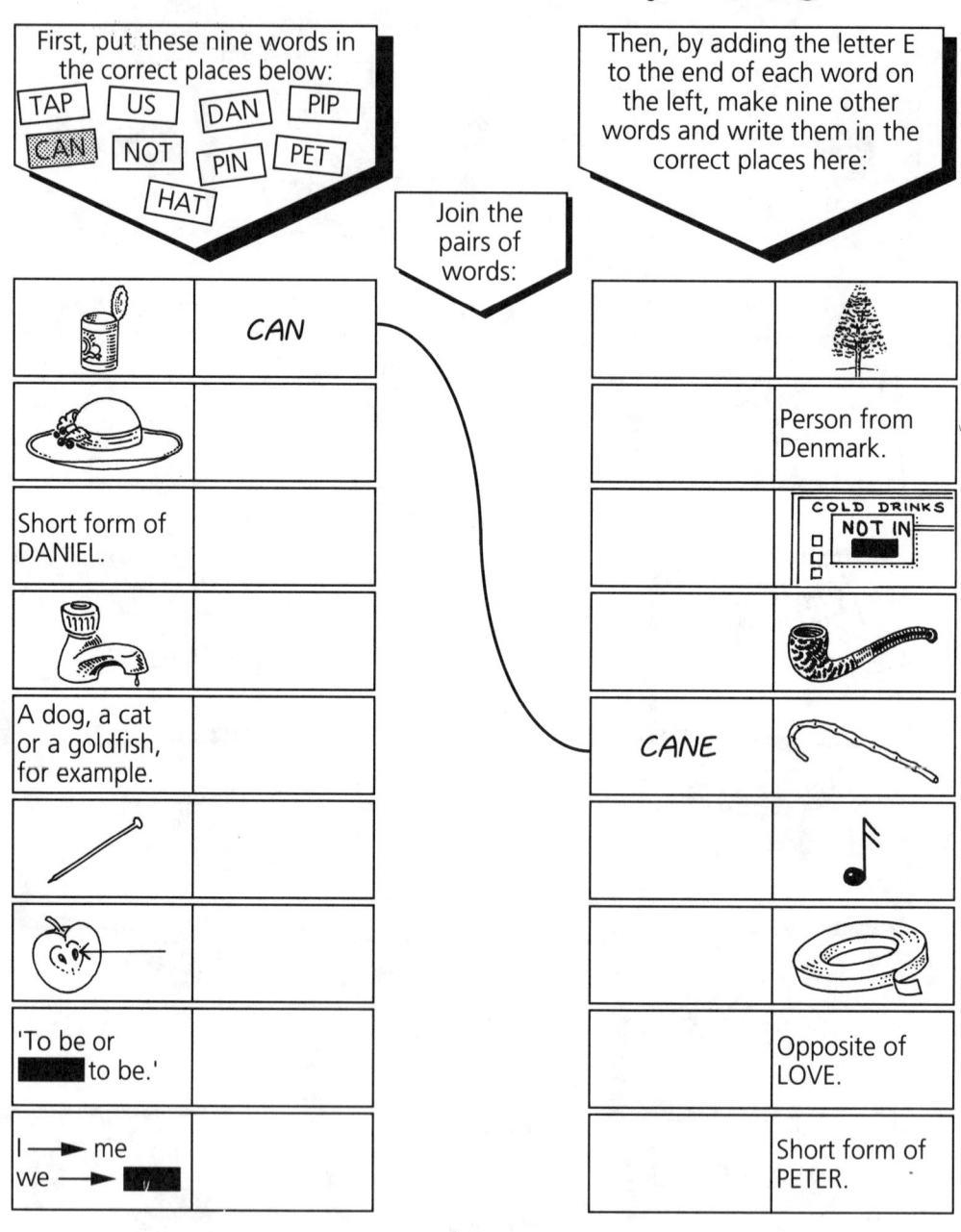

# Pairs of *words*

First, put these nine words in the correct places below:

TAP  US  DAN  PIP  CAN  NOT  PIN  PET  HAT

Then, by adding the letter E to the end of each word on the left, make nine other words and write them in the correct places here:

Join the pairs of words:

| | CAN |
|---|---|
| | |
| Short form of DANIEL. | |
| | |
| A dog, a cat or a goldfish, for example. | |
| | |
| | |
| 'To be or ▇ to be.' | |
| I → me we → ▇ | |

| | |
|---|---|
| | |
| | Person from Denmark. |
| | |
| CANE | |
| | |
| | |
| | Opposite of LOVE. |
| | Short form of PETER. |

**Question:** What is special about the pronunciation of the words in the pairs (*can/cane*, etc.)?

**PUZZLE 10**

English Puzzles 4  Heinemann International

# Abbreviations

Complete the crossword grid by putting in the full forms of the twenty-two abbreviations.

**Envelope 1:**
Dr. Graham Kent
25 Market Sq.
Shakespeare Rd.
Birchester

**Envelope 2:**
Prof. Margaret Baker
Dept. of Linguistics
Churchill Bldg.
Univ. of Birchester
Milton Ave.
Birchester

**Envelope 3:**
The Johnson Computer Co. Ltd.
77-79 King St.
Birchester

Crossword grid with 4 Down starting "DOCTOR".

### SOME WORLD RECORDS
The highest active volcano:
Ojos del Salado, 6885 m. (22588 ft.)
The longest river:
The Nile, 6670 kms. (4145 mls.)
The longest space flight:
Vladimir Titov and Musa Manarov,
365 days 22 hrs. 39 mins. 47 secs.
(21 Dec. 1987 – 21 Dec. 1988)

### A FAMOUS QUOTATION
Big Brother is watching you.
– George Orwell,
  *Nineteen Eighty-Four*,
  Pt. 1, Chap. 1, p. 1

English Puzzles 4   Heinemann International

**PUZZLE 11**

# A Strange quiz

The questions in this quiz are *riddles* – they may appear strange, but they all have logical answers. Find the correct answers in the box, and write them under the questions.

1) What do elephants do when it rains?
___

2) Why do businessmen carry umbrellas?
___

3) What kind of umbrella does a businessman carry when it's raining very hard?
___

4) Twelve businessmen were standing under one small umbrella, but none of them got wet. Why?
___

5) Why did William Shakespeare wear a red and green belt?
___

6) Who wears the biggest boots in the army?
___

7) What can you add to a bucket of water to make it lighter?
___

8) What can fall on water without getting wet?
___

9) How do you stop water coming into your house?
___

10) What kind of lion has purple feet?
___

11) Why do giraffes have long necks?
___

12) Why do white sheep sleep more than black sheep?
___

| | | |
|---|---|---|
| The soldier with the biggest feet. | Because there are more of them. | To join their heads to their bodies. |
| Holes. | Because it wasn't raining. | To keep his trousers up. |
| A very wet one. | Because umbrellas can't walk. | They get wet. |
| The kind that makes its own wine. | A shadow. | Stop paying your water bill. |

**PUZZLE** 12     English Puzzles 4    Heinemann International

# A very official jigsaw

Find a more formal or 'official' way of saying each of these things. You can find the 'official' versions in the jigsaw. The words of each sentence are on pieces which are joined together.

1. WHAT'S YOUR JOB? / WHAT IS YOUR OCCUPATION?
2. ARE YOU MARRIED?
3. HOW OLD ARE YOU?
4. HOW TALL ARE YOU?
5. HOW MUCH DO YOU WEIGH?
6. WHICH COUNTRY DO YOU LIVE IN?
7. WHAT'S YOUR ADDRESS?

Jigsaw pieces:
- WHAT IS YOUR OCCUPATION?
- WHAT IS YOUR COUNTRY OF RESIDENCE?
- WHAT IS YOUR HEIGHT?
- WHAT IS YOUR AGE?
- WHAT IS YOUR MARITAL STATUS?
- WHAT IS YOUR FULL POSTAL ADDRESS?
- WHAT IS YOUR WEIGHT?

English Puzzles 4   Heinemann International

PUZZLE 13

# Grammar FILES

Here are eighteen files. On each file, there is an English grammatical term, but these terms are not written in full. What are the full forms?
For example, ADJ'S means ADJECTIVES, and ADJ'S (POSS.) means ADJECTIVES (POSSESSIVE).

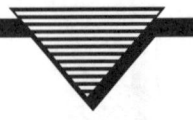

Write the full forms here. (If you have a problem, you can find all the words in the alphabetical list at the bottom of the page.)

Files (labels):
1. ADJ'S
2. ADJ'S (POSS.)
3. ADV'S
4. ART. (DEF.)
5. ART. (INDEF.)
6. CONJ'S
7. NOUNS (UNC.)
8. NOUNS (C., SING.)
9. NOUNS (C., PL.)
10. PREP'S
11. PRON'S (SUBJ.)
12. PRON'S (OBJ.)
13. PRON'S (POSS.)
14. VERBS (REG.): INF.
15. VERBS (IRREG.): INF.
16. VERBS: -ing FM
17. VERBS: PAST SIMP. FM
18. VERBS: PAST PART.

| | List of files |
|---|---|
| 1 | ADJECTIVES |
| 2 | ADJECTIVES (POSSESSIVE) |
| 3 | |
| 4 | |
| 5 | |
| ○ 6 | |
| 7 | |
| 8 | |
| 9 | |
| 10 | |
| 11 | |
| 12 | |
| ○ 13 | |
| 14 | |
| 15 | |
| 16 | |
| 17 | |
| 18 | |

When you have done this puzzle, try the puzzle on the opposite page.

Alphabetical list:
ADJECTIVES
ADVERBS
ARTICLE
CONJUNCTIONS
COUNTABLE
DEFINITE
FORM
INDEFINITE
INFINITIVE
IRREGULAR
OBJECT
PARTICIPLE
PLURAL
POSSESSIVE
PREPOSITIONS
PRONOUNS
REGULAR
SIMPLE
SINGULAR
SUBJECT
UNCOUNTABLE

PUZZLE 14          English Puzzles 4    Heinemann International

# Documents for the FILES

⚠ Do the puzzle on the opposite page before you do this one.

Each of the documents below belongs in one of the files on the opposite page. Read the words on each document and decide where it belongs.
For example: The words *my, your, his, her, its, our* and *their* are Possessive Adjectives, so document A belongs in file 2.

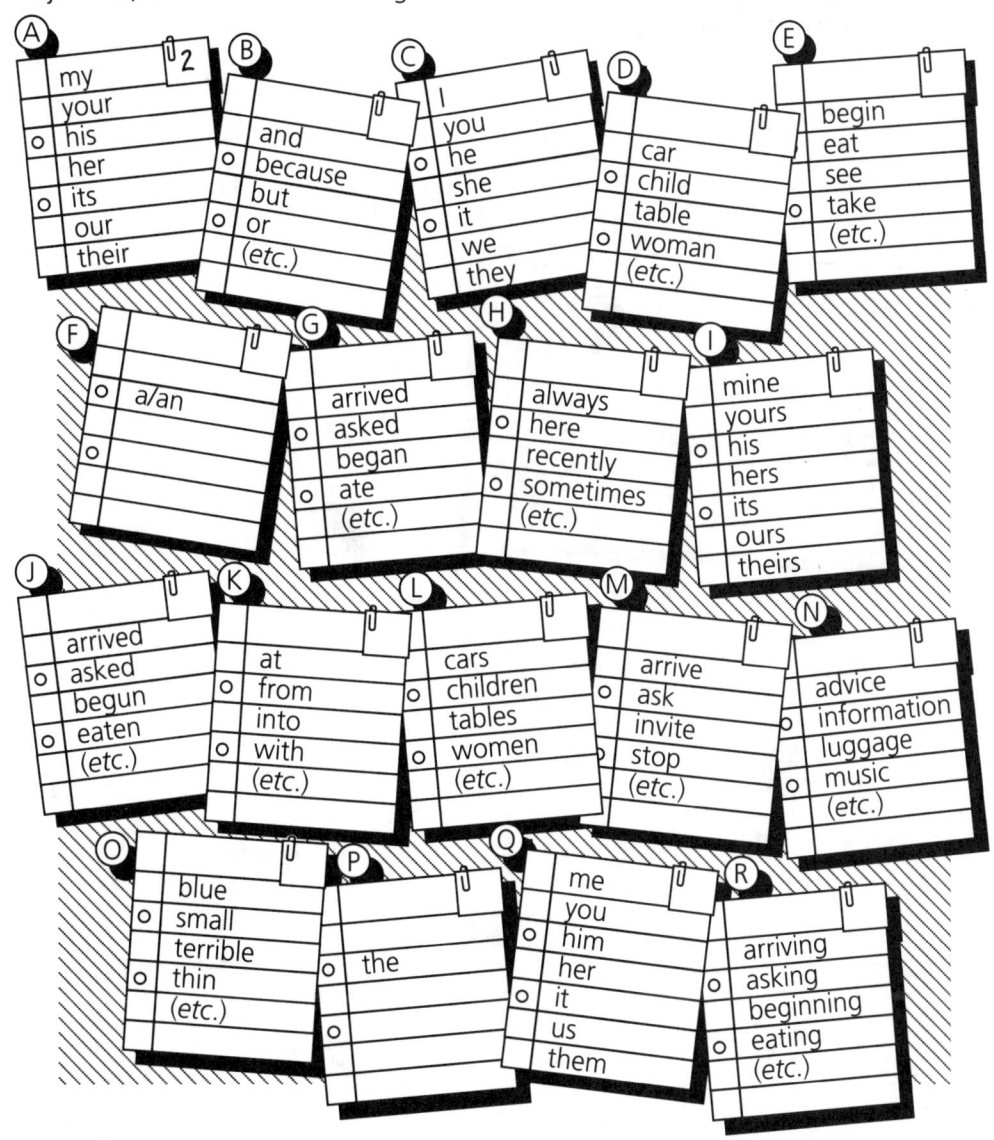

**A** (2)
- my
- your
- his
- her
- its
- our
- their

**B**
- and
- because
- but
- or
- (etc.)

**C**
- I
- you
- he
- she
- it
- we
- they

**D**
- car
- child
- table
- woman
- (etc.)

**E**
- begin
- eat
- see
- take
- (etc.)

**F**
- a/an

**G**
- arrived
- asked
- began
- ate
- (etc.)

**H**
- always
- here
- recently
- sometimes
- (etc.)

**I**
- mine
- yours
- his
- hers
- its
- ours
- theirs

**J**
- arrived
- asked
- begun
- eaten
- (etc.)

**K**
- at
- from
- into
- with
- (etc.)

**L**
- cars
- children
- tables
- women
- (etc.)

**M**
- arrive
- ask
- invite
- stop
- (etc.)

**N**
- advice
- information
- luggage
- music
- (etc.)

**O**
- blue
- small
- terrible
- thin
- (etc.)

**P**
- the

**Q**
- me
- you
- him
- her
- it
- us
- them

**R**
- arriving
- asking
- beginning
- eating
- (etc.)

| Question: | Some of the documents don't have (*etc.*) at the end. Why not?

English Puzzles 4    Heinemann International                                    PUZZLE 15

# Strong feelings

A angry  B furious

In this pair of adjectives, B is *stronger* than A: 'furious' means '*very* angry'.

Find six more pairs of adjectives, and write them in the correct pictures below. (Adjective B is always stronger than Adjective A.) You can find the letters of each adjective in one of the small grids – starting in the middle square and going in one of these directions:

# Telegram LANGUAGE

In this telegram: | ARRIVING GATWICK AIRPORT FRIDAY 10.30. |

these words have been omitted: | I'LL BE | AT | ON | AT |

The complete sentence is:
*I'LL BE* ARRIVING *AT* GATWICK AIRPORT *ON* FRIDAY *AT* 10.30.

'Telegram language' is used in other kinds of writing too. There are some examples in this puzzle.

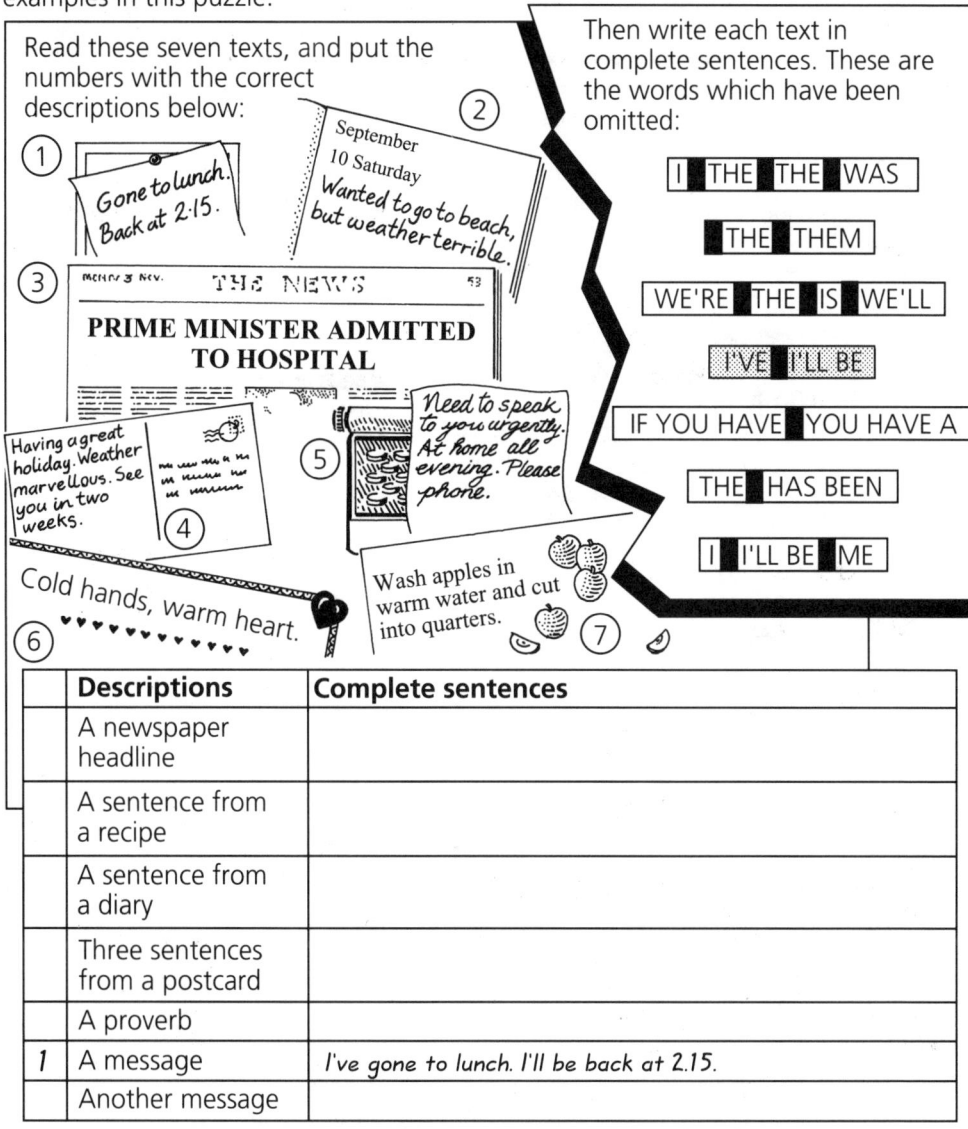

Read these seven texts, and put the numbers with the correct descriptions below:

Then write each text in complete sentences. These are the words which have been omitted:

| I | THE | THE | WAS |
| THE | THEM |
| WE'RE | THE | IS | WE'LL |
| I'VE | I'LL BE |
| IF YOU HAVE | YOU HAVE A |
| THE | HAS BEEN |
| I | I'LL BE | ME |

1. Gone to lunch. Back at 2.15.
2. September 10 Saturday. Wanted to go to beach, but weather terrible.
3. THE NEWS — PRIME MINISTER ADMITTED TO HOSPITAL
4. Having a great holiday. Weather marvellous. See you in two weeks.
5. Need to speak to you urgently. At home all evening. Please phone.
6. Cold hands, warm heart.
7. Wash apples in warm water and cut into quarters.

| | Descriptions | Complete sentences |
|---|---|---|
| | A newspaper headline | |
| | A sentence from a recipe | |
| | A sentence from a diary | |
| | Three sentences from a postcard | |
| | A proverb | |
| 1 | A message | I've gone to lunch. I'll be back at 2.15. |
| | Another message | |

English Puzzles 4  Heinemann International

# Logical laws

Look at these two 'logical laws':

A person with one watch knows what time it is; a person with two watches is never sure.

In the summer, bus windows never open; in the winter, bus windows never close.

Here are eight more 'logical laws'. Work out what the missing words are, and put them into the crossword grid.

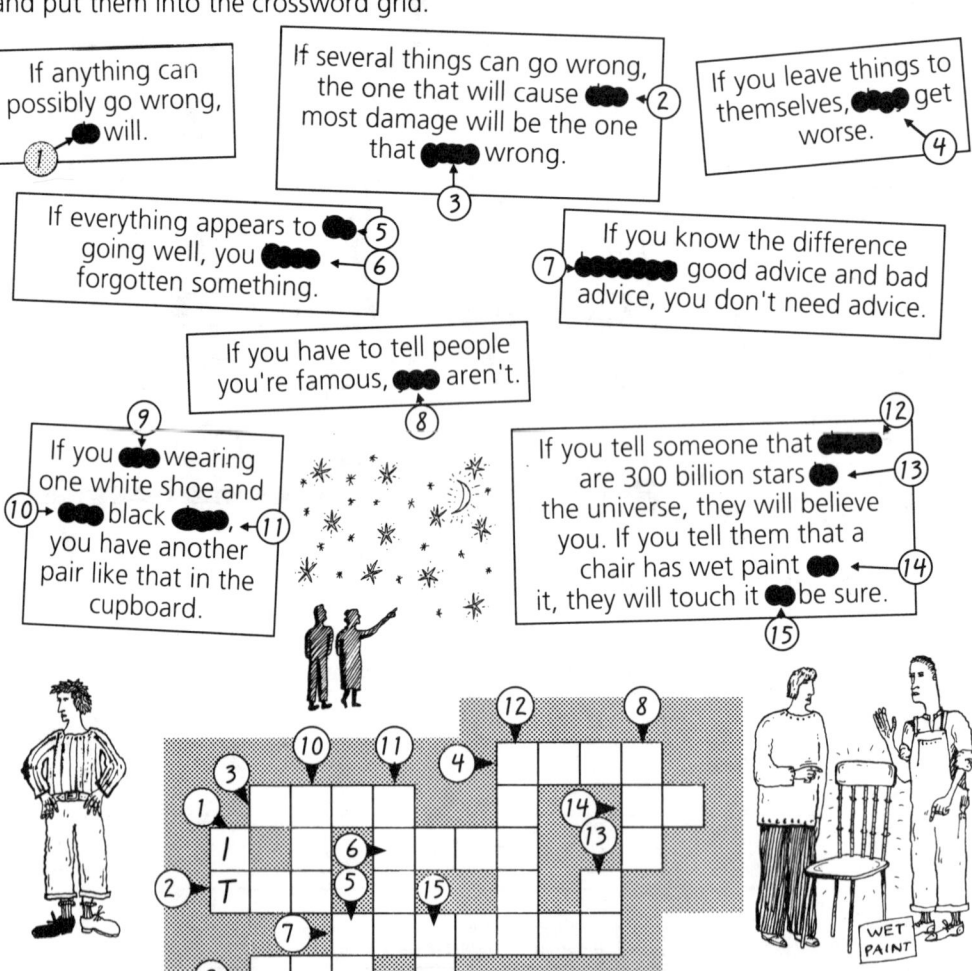

If anything can possibly go wrong, ●● will. (1)

If several things can go wrong, the one that will cause ●●● most damage will be the one (2) that ●●● wrong. (3)

If you leave things to themselves, ●●● get worse. (4)

If everything appears to ●● (5) going well, you ●●● (6) forgotten something.

If you know the difference (7) ●●●●●●● good advice and bad advice, you don't need advice.

If you have to tell people you're famous, ●●● aren't. (8)

If you ●● wearing (9) one white shoe and (10)→ ●●● black ●●●●, ←(11) you have another pair like that in the cupboard.

If you tell someone that ●●●●●● (12) are 300 billion stars ●● ←(13) the universe, they will believe you. If you tell them that a chair has wet paint ●● ←(14) it, they will touch it ●● be sure. (15)

PUZZLE 18                English Puzzles 4    Heinemann International

# At the theatre

With just ten words, you can complete all the titles in this list of plays by British, Irish and American writers.
The clues will help you to discover the ten words.

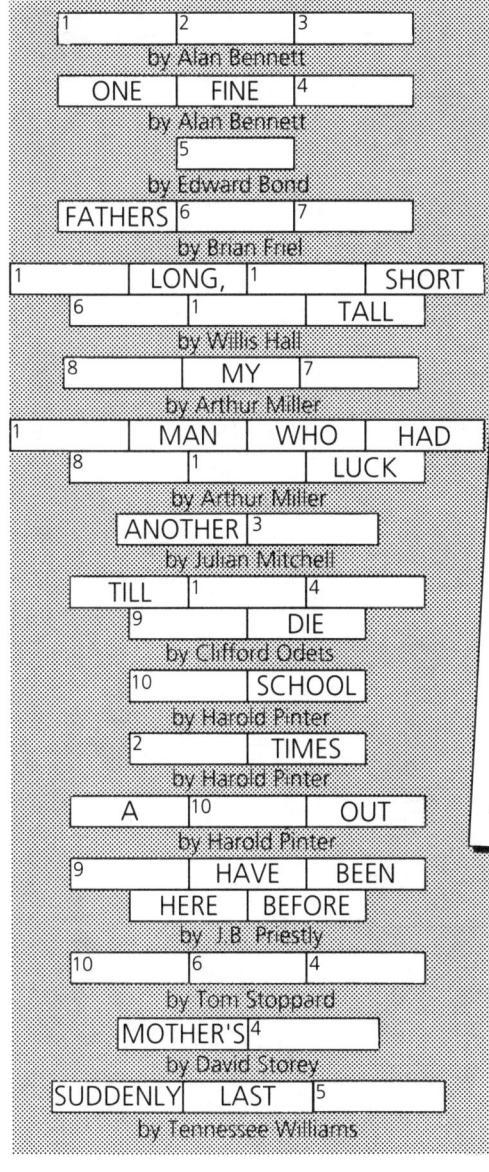

| 1 | 2 | 3 |
by Alan Bennett
| ONE | FINE | 4 |
by Alan Bennett
| 5 |
by Edward Bond
| FATHERS | 6 | 7 |
by Brian Friel
| 1 | LONG, | 1 | SHORT |
| 6 | 1 | TALL |
by Willis Hall
| 8 | MY | 7 |
by Arthur Miller
| 1 | MAN | WHO | HAD |
| 8 | 1 | LUCK |
by Arthur Miller
| ANOTHER | 3 |
by Julian Mitchell
| TILL | 1 | 4 |
| 9 | DIE |
by Clifford Odets
| 10 | SCHOOL |
by Harold Pinter
| 2 | TIMES |
by Harold Pinter
| A | 10 | OUT |
by Harold Pinter
| 9 | HAVE | BEEN |
| HERE | BEFORE |
by J B Priestly
| 10 | 6 | 4 |
by Tom Stoppard
| MOTHER'S | 4 |
by David Storey
| SUDDENLY | LAST | 5 |
by Tennessee Williams

## Clues

1 Definite article (three letters).

2 Adjective, opposite of *young* (three letters).

3 Noun – France, for example, or Brazil, or Japan . . . (seven letters).

4 Noun, a period of twenty-four hours (three letters).

5 Noun, the season when the weather is hot (six letters).

6 Conjunction (three letters).

7 Noun, opposite of *daughters* (four letters).

8 Adjective, opposite of *no* (three letters).

9 Pronoun (one letter).

10 Noun, opposite of *day* (five letters).

English Puzzles 4   Heinemann International

PUZZLE  19

# Disc jockey

The disc jockey is planning to play twelve records. All twelve are about love – a very popular subject for songs! Read his list and complete each song title, using one of these words: **LOVE**, **LOVED**, **LOVING**

|  |  |  |
|---|---|---|
| 1 | DANNY WILSON 1989 | IF YOU REALLY ☐ ME, LET ME GO. |
| 2 | TAYLOR DAYNE 1988 | I'LL ALWAYS ☐ YOU. |
| 3 | A FLOCK OF SEAGULLS 1984 | THE MORE YOU LIVE, THE MORE YOU ☐. |
| 4 | GARY GLITTER 1972 | I DIDN'T KNOW I ☐ YOU, TILL I SAW YOU ROCK'N'ROLL. |
| 5 | MICHAEL JACKSON 1987 | I JUST CAN'T STOP ☐ YOU. |
| 6 | FREDDIE JACKSON 1987 | HAVE YOU EVER ☐ SOMEBODY? |
| 7 | JOAN JETT 1988 | I HATE MYSELF FOR ☐ YOU. |
| 8 | ALEXANDER O'NEAL 1988 | WHAT CAN I SAY TO MAKE YOU ☐ ME? |
| 9 | QUEEN 1976 | SOMEBODY TO ☐. |
| 10 | OTIS REDDING 1966 | I'VE BEEN ☐ YOU TOO LONG. |
| 11 | STING 1988 | IF YOU ☐ SOMEBODY, SET THEM FREE. |
| 12 | THE ZOMBIES 1965 | I REMEMBER WHEN I ☐ HER. |

Questions:

1 In which three titles is the verb *love* in the *Present Simple*?

2 In which two titles is *loved* the *Past Simple*?

3 In which title is *loved* part of the *Present Perfect*?

4 Which title is in the *Present Perfect Continuous*?

PUZZLE 20      English Puzzles 4      Heinemann International

# House and garden

Label the parts of the house and garden. The letters you need for each thing are given, but not in the correct order.

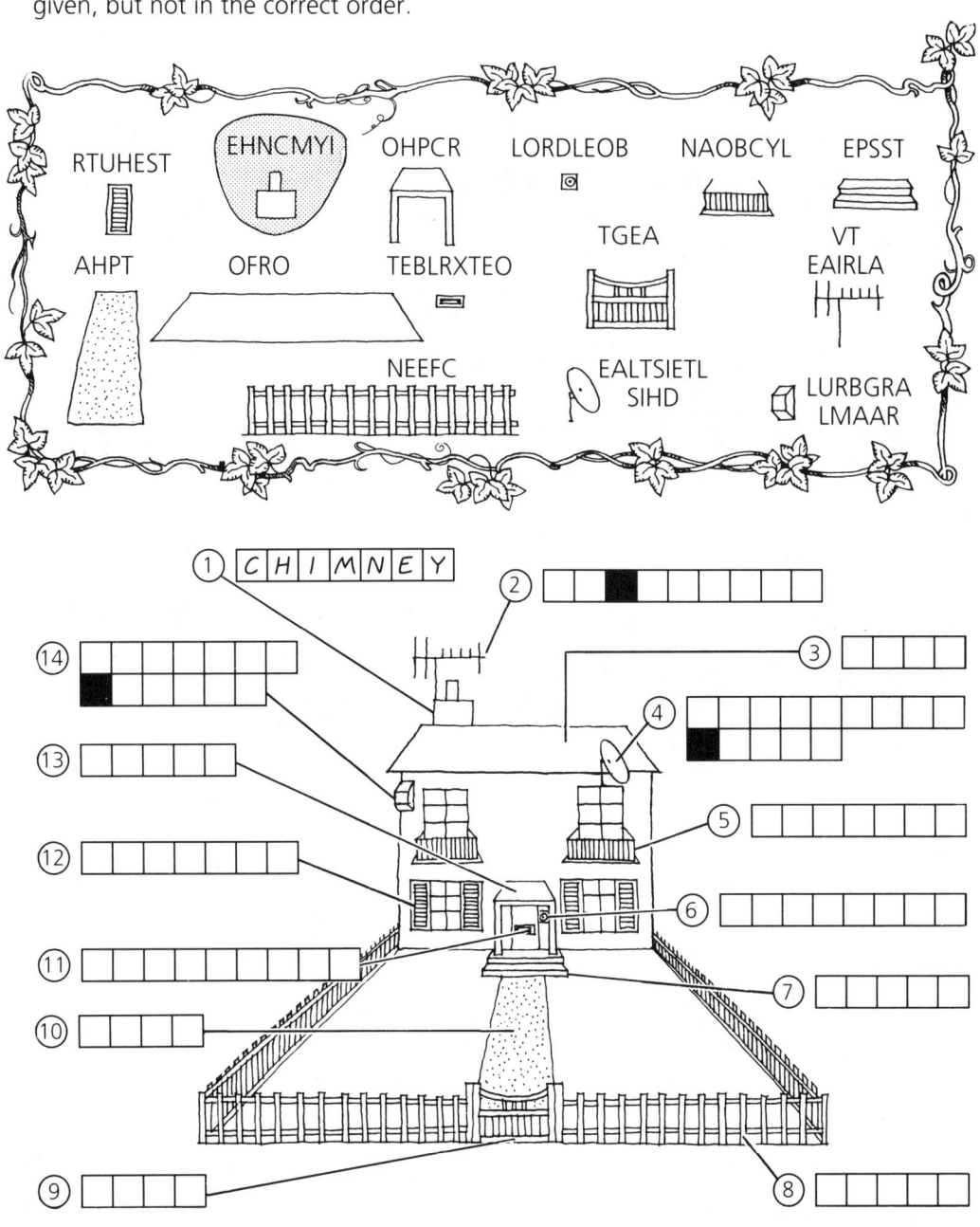

RTUHEST  EHNCMYI  OHPCR  LORDLEOB  NAOBCYL  EPSST

AHPT  OFRO  TEBLRXTEO  TGEA  VT EAIRLA

NEEFC  EALTSIETL SIHD  LURBGRA LMAAR

1. C H I M N E Y

English Puzzles 4   Heinemann International

PUZZLE 21

# What do they *really* mean?

Find the correct meaning for each of these road signs, and write it instead of the incorrect meaning. All the correct meanings are in the box at the bottom of the page. For example, the first sign doesn't *really* mean 'Danger: Sausages in road'. It means 'Roundabout'.

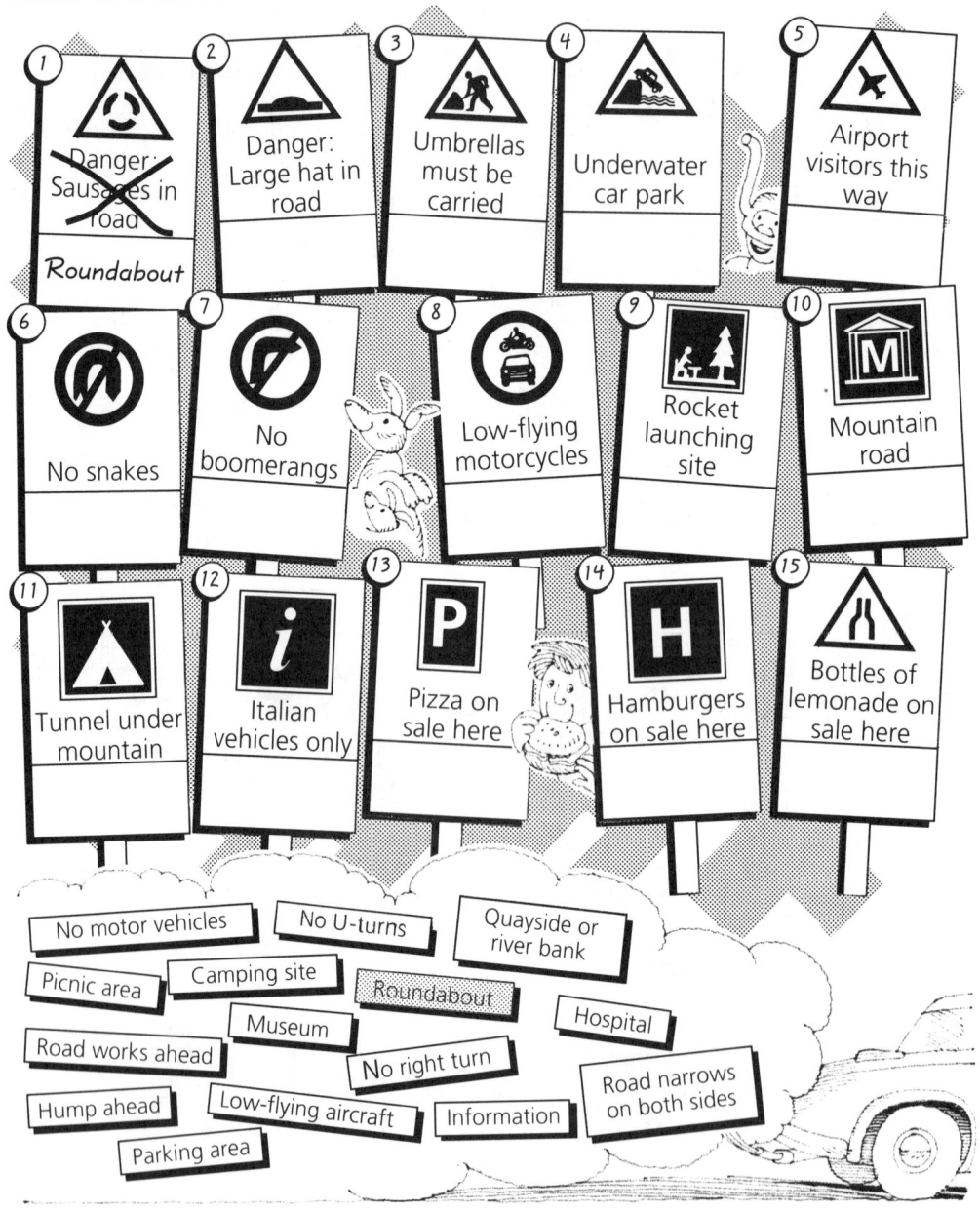

1. ~~Danger: Sausages in Road~~ *Roundabout*
2. Danger: Large hat in road
3. Umbrellas must be carried
4. Underwater car park
5. Airport visitors this way
6. No snakes
7. No boomerangs
8. Low-flying motorcycles
9. Rocket launching site
10. Mountain road
11. Tunnel under mountain
12. Italian vehicles only
13. Pizza on sale here
14. Hamburgers on sale here
15. Bottles of lemonade on sale here

No motor vehicles · No U-turns · Quayside or river bank · Picnic area · Camping site · Roundabout · Museum · Hospital · Road works ahead · No right turn · Road narrows on both sides · Hump ahead · Low-flying aircraft · Information · Parking area

PUZZLE 22

English Puzzles 4    Heinemann International

# Interesting facts

The nine interesting facts below (A–I) include fourteen numbers. Write these numbers in figures, and then add them all together. The total will give you the number which is missing from the other interesting fact (J).

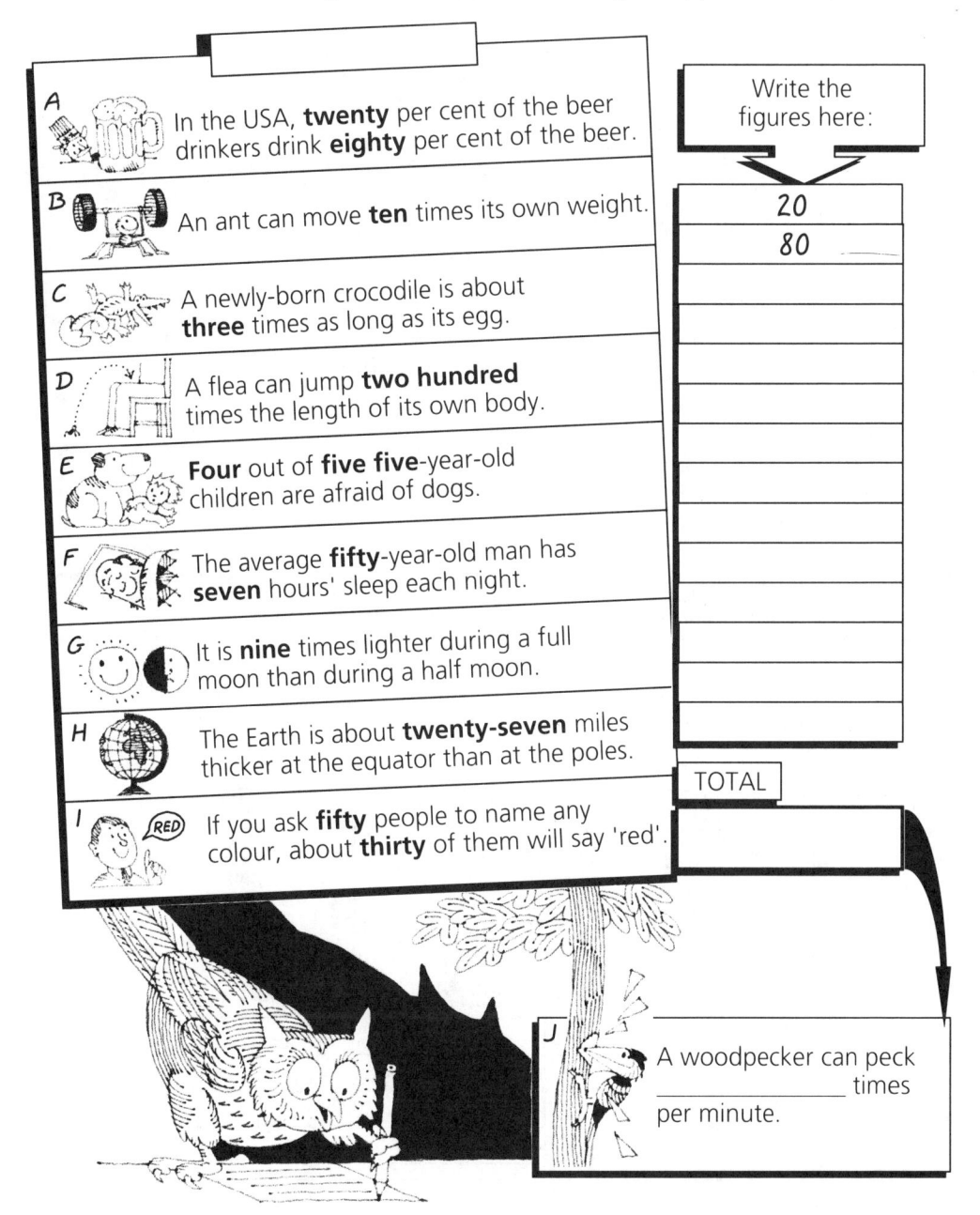

Write the figures here:

A  In the USA, **twenty** per cent of the beer drinkers drink **eighty** per cent of the beer.

| 20 |
| 80 |

B  An ant can move **ten** times its own weight.

C  A newly-born crocodile is about **three** times as long as its egg.

D  A flea can jump **two hundred** times the length of its own body.

E  **Four** out of **five** five-year-old children are afraid of dogs.

F  The average **fifty**-year-old man has **seven** hours' sleep each night.

G  It is **nine** times lighter during a full moon than during a half moon.

H  The Earth is about **twenty-seven** miles thicker at the equator than at the poles.

I  If you ask **fifty** people to name any colour, about **thirty** of them will say 'red'.

TOTAL

J  A woodpecker can peck _____ times per minute.

English Puzzles 4    Heinemann International

PUZZLE 23

# Folded paper

This piece of paper has a song title written on it, but because it is folded, the first two words are hidden:

NIGHT (Phil Collins, 1985)

If the piece of unfolded, you can read the complete title:

ONE MORE NIGHT (Phil Collins, 1985)

Here are some more pieces of paper with song titles written on them. What are the two hidden words on each piece of paper?

1. GAMES (Maze, 1985)
2. TROUBLE (Limahl, 1984)
3. US (Abba, 1981)
4. US ARE SAD (The Eagles, 1972)
5. MINUTE (Matt Bianco, 1984)
6. SATURDAY NIGHT (Matchbox, 1982)
7. LONELY NIGHTS (Paul McCartney, 1984)

These are the words you need:

ONE OF
ONE MORE
MOST OF
NO MORE
HALF A
TOO MANY
TOO MUCH

Write the complete song titles here:

| 1 | TOO MANY GAMES | 5 | |
| 2 | | 6 | |
| 3 | | 7 | |
| 4 | | | |

There are also two hidden words in each of these film titles. What are they?

A. OUR AIRCRAFT IS MISSING (UK, 1941)
B. RIVER (US, 1934)
C. A MILLION (US, 1936)
D. ONE (US, 1974)

ONE MORE
ONE IN
ONE BY
ONE OF

Write the complete film titles here:

| A | |
| B | |
| C | |
| D | |

**PUZZLE** 24

English Puzzles 4    Heinemann International

# What are they saying?

First, put each of these eight sentences into the correct picture. (Don't worry about the numbers under the pictures for the moment.)

- I haven't been feeling very well recently, doctor.
- How long have you been working on it?
- Have you been waiting long?
- We've been looking forward to this holiday for months.
- It's been raining all morning.
- It's been doing that all morning.
- How long have you been studying Chinese?
- You've been working too hard.

A: 7 14 34 36 40 55 61 69

B: 2 15 20 28 33 46 58 66

C: 5 18 24 30 44 48 52 68

D: 9 13 27 31 43 47 50 60

E: 6 17 23 29 38 45 54 62

F: 4 10 16 32 37 51 57 65

G: 1 12 35 39 53 59 63 67

H: 3 11 22 26 42 49 56 64

Now look at the numbers under the pictures in which the speakers are **asking questions**. Fill in the letters below which have those numbers, and the name of a tense will appear.

English Puzzles 4    Heinemann International

PUZZLE 25

# THE SECOND HALF

Look at these two titles – each has two halves:

UPSTAIRS, DOWNSTAIRS (British TV programme)

ANOTHER TIME, ANOTHER PLACE (Film)

Now look at the titles of the nine books below. (The books are by writers from the United States, the United Kingdom, Australia and France.) The first two titles are complete, but in each of the others *the second half* is missing. Complete the titles, using the words in the alphabetical list.

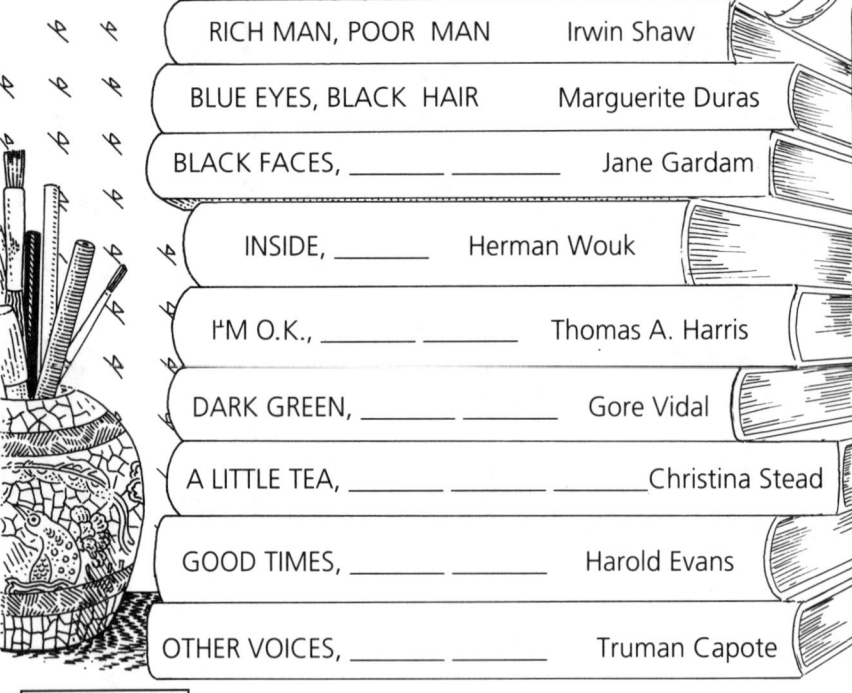

| RICH MAN, POOR MAN | Irwin Shaw |
| BLUE EYES, BLACK HAIR | Marguerite Duras |
| BLACK FACES, _____ _____ | Jane Gardam |
| INSIDE, _____ | Herman Wouk |
| I'M O.K., _____ _____ | Thomas A. Harris |
| DARK GREEN, _____ _____ | Gore Vidal |
| A LITTLE TEA, _____ _____ _____ | Christina Stead |
| GOOD TIMES, _____ _____ | Harold Evans |
| OTHER VOICES, _____ _____ | Truman Capote |

A
BAD
BRIGHT
CHAT
FACES
LITTLE
O.K.
OTHER
OUTSIDE
RED
ROOMS
TIMES
WHITE
YOU'RE

Questions:

All of the books are *novels* except two. These two are (A) a book about psychology, and (B) an autobiography. Which book is (A)? And which book is (B)? You can find the answers with the help of these clues:
– *The book about psychology* is the only one with apostrophes in its title.
– *The autobiography* was written by an editor of 'The Times' newspaper.

PUZZLE 26        English Puzzles 4    Heinemann International

# Grammatical terms

Do you know these nine grammatical terms? They describe sentences, words and their parts.

SENTENCE  WORD  SYLLABLE  VOWEL  PREFIX
PHRASE  LETTER  CONSONANT  SUFFIX

Write those terms in the correct places on this diagram. (You'll need to write them in their plural form.)

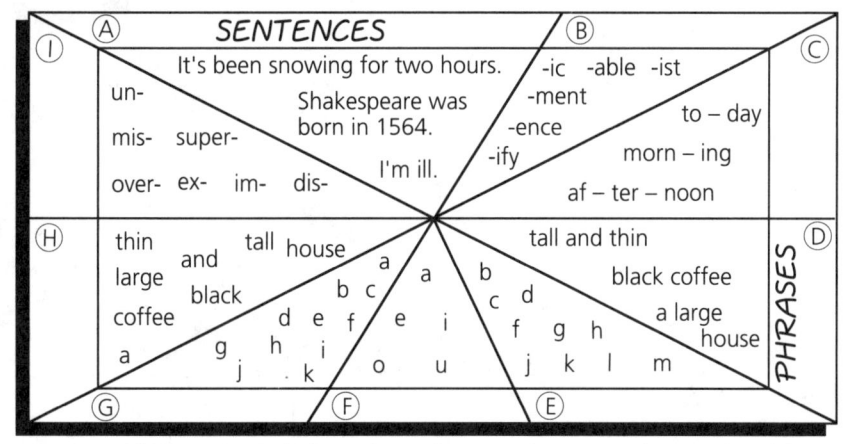

```
       Ⓐ         SENTENCES        Ⓑ
  ①                                              Ⓒ
        It's been snowing for two hours.
       un-                          -ic  -able  -ist
            Shakespeare was       -ment
       mis-  super-  born in 1564.              to – day
                                   -ence
       over-  ex-  im-  dis-  I'm ill.  -ify   morn – ing
                                         af – ter – noon
  Ⓗ                                              Ⓓ
       thin      tall   house                tall and thin
            and                  a
       large         a      b  c    a   b    black coffee
            black                       c  d
       coffee        d   e  f     e   i    f  g   a large
                                                  h  house       PHRASES
       a      g  h   i           o   u     j  k  l  m
                   j    . k
       Ⓖ             Ⓕ              Ⓔ
```

Use the terms to fill the spaces below. (Use them in their singular or plural form, as necessary.)

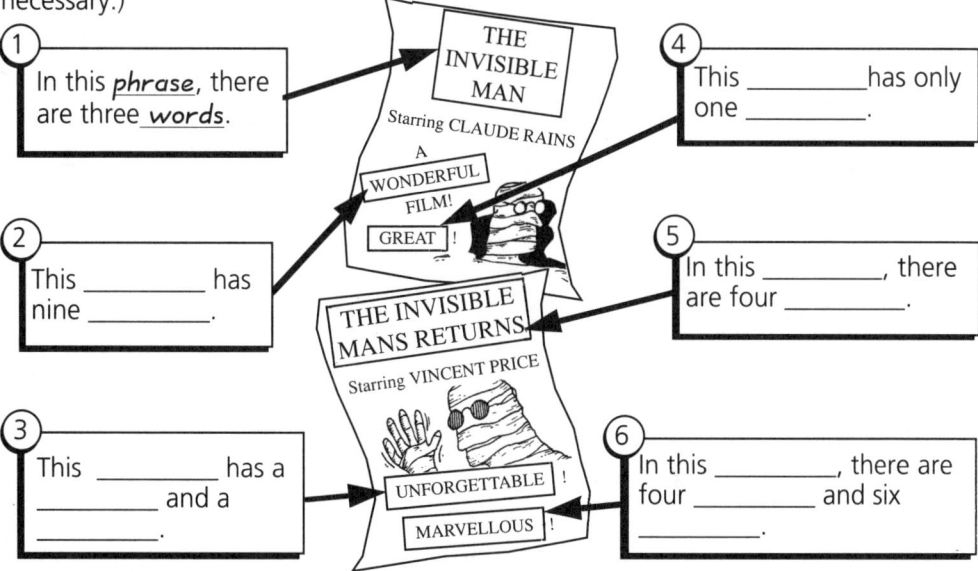

1. In this *phrase*, there are three *words*.

2. This _____ has nine _____.

3. This _____ has a _____ and a _____.

4. This _____ has only one _____.

5. In this _____, there are four _____.

6. In this _____, there are four _____ and six _____.

THE INVISIBLE MAN
Starring CLAUDE RAINS
A WONDERFUL FILM!
GREAT!

THE INVISIBLE MANS RETURNS
Starring VINCENT PRICE
UNFORGETTABLE!
MARVELLOUS!

English Puzzles 4   Heinemann International                    PUZZLE 27

# Shopping list

First, put the missing letters into the words in these pictures. (All the missing letters are vowels: A, E, I, O, U.)

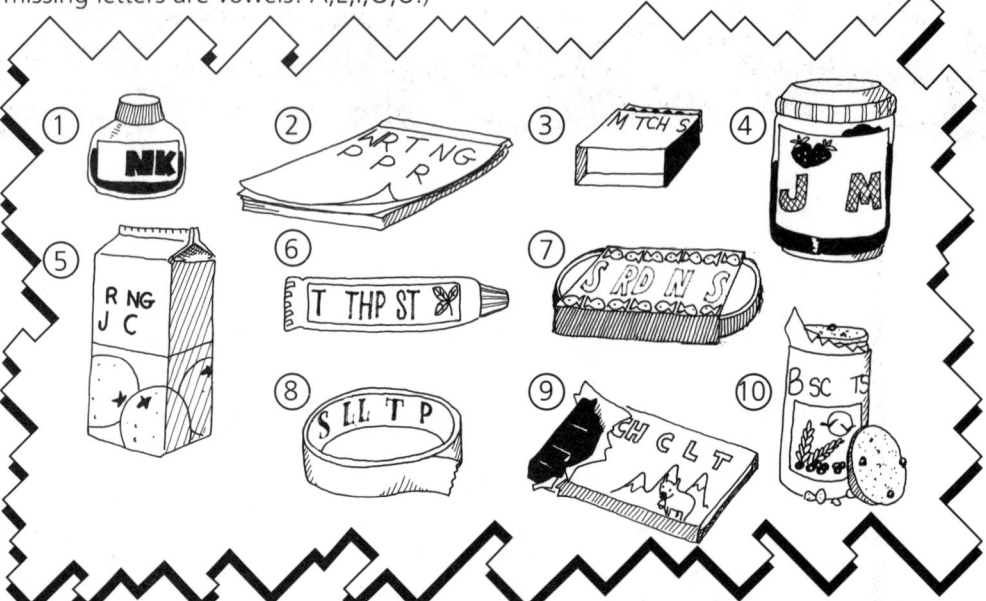

1. NK
2. WR T NG P P R
3. M TCH S
4. J M
5. R NG J C
6. T THP ST
7. S R D N S
8. S LL T P
9. CH C L T
10. B SC TS

Those ten words are on this shopping list, but they are hidden because the list has been folded in half.

Write the complete shopping list here:

**SHOPPING L**
a packet of
a tube of
a tin of
a bottle of
a jar of
a box of
a carton of
a bar of
a roll of
a pad of

PUZZLE 28          English Puzzles 4    Heinemann International

# More logical laws

In Puzzle 18, there are ten 'logical laws'. Here is another one:

> It always starts raining as soon as you decide to leave your umbrella at home.

In the table below, there are ten more 'logical laws', but the first part of each one is with the wrong second part. For example, **You always think of something else to write in a letter as soon as the mechanic arrives to repair it** doesn't make sense.

For each first part, find the correct second part. Write the numbers with the correct letters.

| | | | |
|---|---|---|---|
| A | You always think of something else to write in a letter | as soon as the mechanic arrives to repair it. | 1 |
| B | You always see something marvellous to photograph | as soon as you decide to take a taxi. | 2 |
| C | A machine which was not working always begins working perfectly | just after you have finished the film in your camera. | 3 |
| D | The telephone always rings | when the cabin crew begin serving coffee. | 4 |
| E | If you get out of the bath to answer the telephone, it always stops ringing | before the person who doesn't snore. | 5 |
| F | An aeroplane always encounters turbulence | immediately after the guarantee expires. | 6 |
| G | A toothache always gets better | while you're having a bath. | 7 |
| H | A new car always breaks down | just before you reach it. | 8 |
| I | In a couple, the person who snores always falls asleep | as soon as you have sealed the envelope. | 9 |
| J | The bus you have been waiting for always arrives | as soon as you sit down in the dentist's chair. | 10 |

| | | | |
|---|---|---|---|
| A | 9 | F | |
| B | | G | |
| C | | H | |
| D | | I | |
| E | | J | |

English Puzzles 4    Heinemann International

# A very polite jigsaw

The replies in these nine conversations are not very polite. Find a polite way of saying each one. All the polite sentences you need are in the jigsaw. The words of each sentence are on pieces which are joined together.

**1.** I HAVE AN APPOINTMENT WITH MR. JOHNSON. — SIT DOWN. / PLEASE TAKE A SEAT.

**2.** SHALL I MAKE SOME SPAGHETTI? — I DON'T LIKE SPAGHETTI.

**3.** IS MR. JOHNSON READY TO SEE ME? — WAIT A MINUTE.

**4.** WOULD YOU LIKE TO COME TO MY PARTY ON SATURDAY? — NO.

**5.** DO YOU MIND IF I SMOKE? — YES, I **DO** MIND.

**6.** ARE YOU FREE THIS EVENING? — NO.

**7.** WHICH WOULD YOU PREFER – TEA OR COFFEE? — I DON'T CARE.

**8.** DO YOU LIKE JAZZ? — NOT MUCH.

**9.** I'D LIKE TO SEE MR. JOHNSON. — HE'S OUT.

### Jigsaw pieces

| PLEASE | I'D | RATHER | YOU | I | DON'T | REALLY |
| TAKE | A | I'M | DIDN'T | I'D | LOVE | LIKE |
| JUST | SEAT | AFRAID | HE'S | OUT | TO | SPAGHETTI |
| A | I | DON'T | NOT | I'M | BUT | I |
| MOMENT | PLEASE | MIND | REALLY | AFRAID | NOT | CAN'T |

PUZZLE 30     English Puzzles 4    Heinemann International

# Titles and *authors*

There is a type of English joke (very popular with children) which consists of an invented book title and author.
When you read the author's name aloud, it sounds the same as a phrase or sentence; the phrase or sentence has a connection with the title of the book.
Here are two examples:

**SOLITUDE** by I. Malone

*I. Malone* sounds the same as 'I'm alone'.

**ON THE ROAD** by Laurie Driver

*Laurie Driver* sounds the same as 'lorry driver'.

Write one of these eight authors' names on each of the books below, and add the 'explanations':

Anne Tarktik   Justin Tyme   I. Scream   R.U. Frightened
C. Shorr   Will U.B. There   Stan Dupp   Sue Perstishen

(Remember to read the names aloud, so that you can hear what they sound like.)

**A HOT DAY IN SUMMER** by I. Scream — *I. Scream* sounds the same as *ice-cream.*

**THE SOUTH POLE** by — sounds the same as

**HORROR STORIES** by — sounds the same as

**ON THE BEACH** by — sounds the same as

**THE JUDGE HAS JUST COME IN** by — sounds the same as

**DON'T BE LATE!** by — sounds the same as

**DO BLACK CATS BRING GOOD LUCK?** by — sounds the same as

**THERE'S A PARTY ON SATURDAY** by — sounds the same as

English Puzzles 4   Heinemann International

# TYPING MISTAKES

**1** The letters E, T and A are the most frequent letters in English texts. In this text, they have all been replaced by the letter X. Work out what the text says, and write it correctly on a piece of paper.

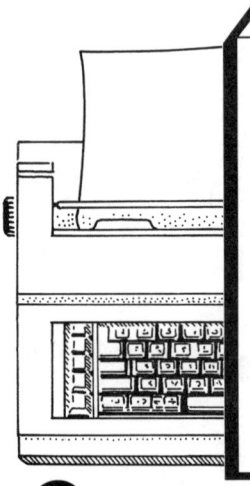

```
                                    75 Norxh Squxrx
                                    Clifdon CL31 7PR
Xhx Royxl Hoxxl                     Novxmbxr 25xh 1991
Church Roxd
Hillborough HI25 7RJ

Dxxr Sir/Mxdxm
Plxxsx rxsxrvx in my nxmx x singlx room wixh
bxxh/showxr for xhx nighx of Wxdnxsdxy Dxcxmbxr
18xh.
Plxxsx xlso lxt mx know whxxhxr you xllow dogs
in xhx hoxxl, xs minx will probxbly bx xrxvxlling
wixh mx.
Yours fxixhfully
John Smith
John Smixh
```

**2** This text is the reply to the text above. It has twelve typing mistakes in it. Find them and correct them.

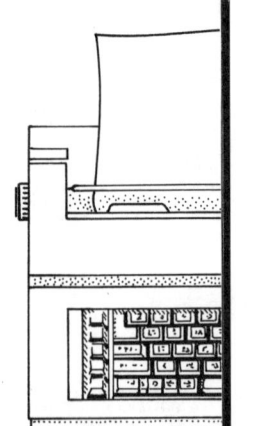

```
                 THE ROYAL HOTEL
        CHURCH ROAD   HILLBOROUGH   HI25 7RJ

Mr John Smith                  November 27th 1991
75 North Square
Clifdon CL31 7PR

Dear Mr Smith
Think you for your letter off November 25th.
I have been a hotel managor for fourty years, and
have never had any problems with dogs.
- Dogs have never fallen asleeep with cigarettes in
  in their hands and burnt their beds.
- Dogs have never stolen towels from there rooms.
- Dogs have never payd their bils with bad cheques.
Your dog will be welcome.
Yours sincerely
J.T.Brown
J.T.Brown
Manager
P.S. If your dog promises that you wil not cause
any problems, you will be wellcome two.
```

PUZZLE 32                    English Puzzles 4   Heinemann International

# THE WORLD CUP

The diagram shows the quarter-finals, the semi-finals and the final of the World Cup football competition in 1990. With the help of the clues, write in all the missing teams and scores. (You don't have to *remember* what happened in the matches – you can work out all the missing teams and scores from the clues.)

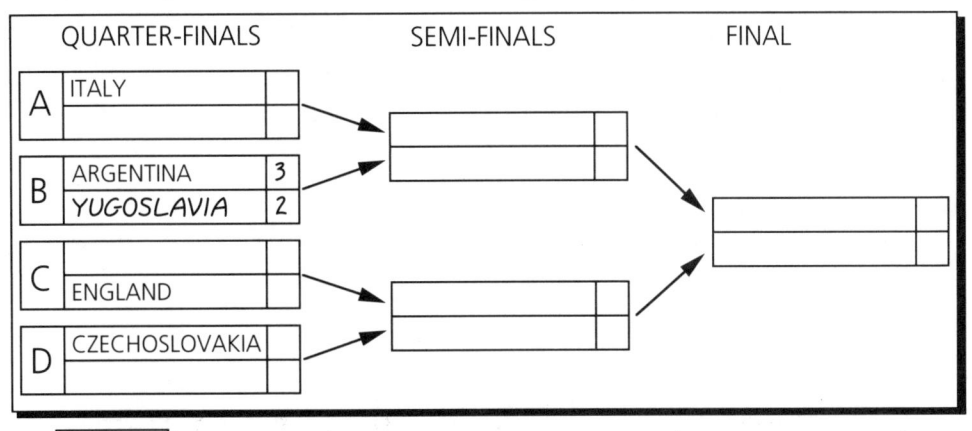

| QUARTER-FINALS | SEMI-FINALS | FINAL |
|---|---|---|
| A | ITALY | | | | | | |
| B | ARGENTINA 3 / YUGOSLAVIA 2 | | | | | | |
| C | ENGLAND | | | | | | |
| D | CZECHOSLOVAKIA | | | | | | |

### Clues

Argentina beat Yugoslavia by three goals to two in Quarter-final B.

West Germany beat Czechoslovakia one-nil in Quarter-final D.

In Quarter-final A, Italy beat Ireland by one goal to nil.

In Quarter-final C, Cameroon lost to England by two goals to three.

In the Semi-finals, the team who won Quarter-final B beat the team who won Quarter-final A by five goals to four. And, by the same score, the team who won Quarter-final D beat the team who won Quarter-final C.

The score in the final was one-nil: the winning team had beaten Czechoslovakia and England on their way to the final.

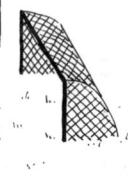

English Puzzles 4   Heinemann International

**PUZZLE 33**

# HOTEL ROOMS

This hotel has forty-eight rooms, and in each room there is a word.

| 801 BILL | 802 PRICE | 803 I'M | 804 HAVE | 805 PHONE | 806 BREAKFAST |
|---|---|---|---|---|---|
| 701 ROOM? | 702 I | 703 SINGLE | 704 A | 705 DO | 706 DIDN'T |
| 601 IN | 602 NOT | 603 IS | 604 WHAT'S | 605 BILL. | 606 ROOM |
| 501 HAVE | 502 YOU | 503 MY | 504 CHECKING | 505 CAN | 506 COULD |
| 401 THE | 402 MAKE | 403 FOR | 404 HAVE | 405 I | 406 PER |
| 301 YOU | 302 BREAKFAST | 303 THERE'S | 304 DO | 305 TOMORROW. | 306 ANY |
| 201 A | 202 MY | 203 NIGHT? | 204 CALLS. | 205 DISTURB | 206 INCLUDED? |
| 101 READY? | 102 IN | 103 OUT | 104 MISTAKE | 105 TONIGHT? | 106 MY |

The words in this group of rooms: (205) (602) (705)
are: DISTURB  NOT  DO
If you put them in the right order, they make a sign you might hang on your hotel room door: DO NOT DISTURB

Do the same with the eight groups of rooms below. The words make four questions you might ask at the reception desk when you arrive, and then four things you might say when you are going to leave.

A (105) (201) (304) (403) (502) (606) (703) (804)
B (203) (401) (406) (604) (802)
C (206) (302) (603)
D (102) (501) (503) (505) (701) (702) (806)
E (103) (305) (504) (803)
F (101) (106) (301) (404) (506) (801)
G (104) (202) (303) (601) (605) (704)
H (204) (306) (402) (405) (706) (805)

PUZZLE 34                English Puzzles 4   Heinemann International

# BRICKS IN A WALL

Each of these pairs of bricks has a sentence written on it. (Each sentence includes an adverbial particle: *in, out, away*, etc.)
Put the pairs of bricks in the correct places in the wall.

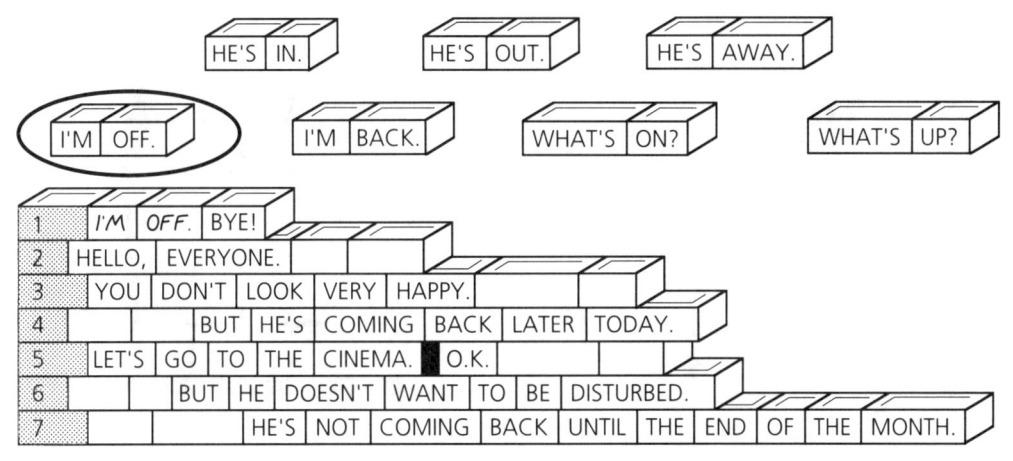

| HE'S | IN. |
| HE'S | OUT. |
| HE'S | AWAY. |
| I'M | OFF. |
| I'M | BACK. |
| WHAT'S | ON? |
| WHAT'S | UP? |

1. I'M OFF. BYE!
2. HELLO, EVERYONE.
3. YOU DON'T LOOK VERY HAPPY.
4. BUT HE'S COMING BACK LATER TODAY.
5. LET'S GO TO THE CINEMA. O.K.
6. BUT HE DOESN'T WANT TO BE DISTURBED.
7. HE'S NOT COMING BACK UNTIL THE END OF THE MONTH.

Now put the numbers into the correct pictures.

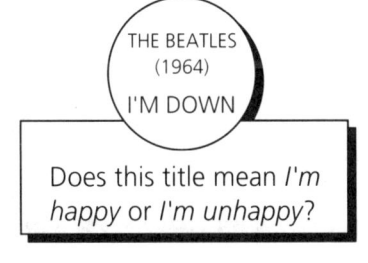

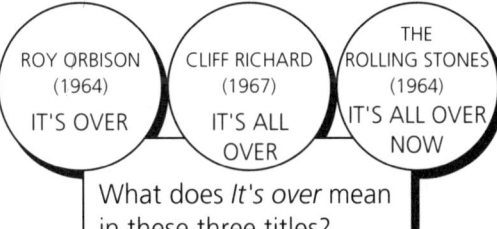

| Questions: | These song titles also have adverbial particles in them.

THE BEATLES (1964)
I'M DOWN

Does this title mean *I'm happy* or *I'm unhappy*?

ROY ORBISON (1964)
IT'S OVER

CLIFF RICHARD (1967)
IT'S ALL OVER

THE ROLLING STONES (1964)
IT'S ALL OVER NOW

What does *It's over* mean in these three titles?

English Puzzles 4   Heinemann International

# A *phonetic* crossword

Here are the 26 letters of the alphabet, with their pronunciation shown in phonetic symbols.

In this crossword, all the answers are abbreviations, like *GB* (for *Great Britain*). The clues are the abbreviations written in phonetic symbols.

### Across

1 /dʒiː/biː/
4 /viː/aɪ/piː/
6 /ɑːr/eɪ/ef/
8 /em/piː/
11 /biː/biː/siː/
13 /juː/es/eɪ/
14 /es/ef/
15 /əʊ/eɪ/juː/
17 /ɑːr/es/viː/piː/

### Down

2 /biː/ɑːr/
3 /el/eɪ/
5 /iː/siː/
7 /ef/biː/aɪ/
9 /piː/tiː/əʊ/
10 /juː/es/es/ɑːr/
11 /biː/eɪ/
12 /siː/aɪ/eɪ/
13 /juː/ef/əʊ/
16 /juː/en/

A /eɪ/   P /piː/
B /biː/   Q /kjuː/
C /siː/   R /ɑːr/
D /diː/   S /es/
E /iː/   T /tiː/
F /ef/   U /juː/
G /dʒiː/  V /viː/
H /eɪtʃ/  W /dʌblju:/
I /aɪ/    X /eks/
J /dʒeɪ/  Y /waɪ/
K /keɪ/   Z /zed/
L /el/    or, in the
M /em/    United
N /en/    States, /ziː/
O /əʊ/

Here are the complete forms of the abbreviations in the crossword. For each one, write the correct number and *Across* or *Down*.

| | | | |
|---|---|---|---|
| British Airways | | Please turn over | |
| British Broadcasting Corporation | | Royal Air Force | |
| | | Please reply (from the French: *Répondez s'il vous plaît*) | |
| British Rail | | | |
| Central Intelligence Agency | | Science fiction | |
| European Community | | Unidentified Flying Object | |
| Federal Bureau of Investigation | | United Nations | |
| Great Britain | 1 Across | United States of America | |
| Los Angeles | | | |
| Member of Parliament | | Union of Soviet Socialist Republics | |
| Organization of African Unity | | Very important person | |

PUZZLE 36                English Puzzles 4    Heinemann International

# KNOCK! KNOCK!

There is a popular type of English joke, called a 'Knock! Knock!' joke. Here is an example:

> A: Knock! Knock!
> B: Who's there?
> A: Frank.
> B: Frank who?
> A: Frank you very much.

This is how it works:

- Person A says: *Knock! Knock!*
- Person B says: *Who's there?*
- Person A says a name.
- Person B says the name and *who?*
- Person A says a sentence beginning with a word (or words) sounding like the name.
  In this example, *Frank* /fræŋk/ sounds like *Thank* /θæŋk/ in *Thank you very much*.

Put each of these names into one of the 'Knock! Knock!' jokes below. If you have a problem, there is some help at the bottom of the page.

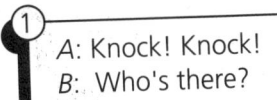

Betty   Ken   Harry   Mary   Howard   Paul

**1**
> A: Knock! Knock!
> B: Who's there?
> A: ..........
> B: .......... who?
> A: .......... I come in?

**2**
> A: Knock! Knock!
> B: Who's there?
> A: ..........
> B: .......... who?
> A: .......... up and open the door!

**3**
> A: Knock! Knock!
> B: Who's there?
> A: ..........
> B: .......... who?
> A: .......... Christmas!

**4**
> A: Knock! Knock!
> B: Who's there?
> A: ..........
> B: .......... who?
> A: .......... I know!

**5**
> A: Knock! Knock!
> B: Who's there?
> A: ..........
> B: .......... who?
> A: .......... harder and maybe the door will open.

**6**
> A: Knock! Knock!
> B: Who's there?
> A: ..........
> B: .......... who?
> A: .......... late than never!

The six names sound like these words:

PULL   CAN   HURRY   BETTER   HOW WOULD   MERRY

English Puzzles 4   Heinemann International

# On the telephone

Put the missing words from the conversations into the grid, vertically. If you complete the grid correctly, the job of one of the people in the pictures will appear in the special squares, horizontally.

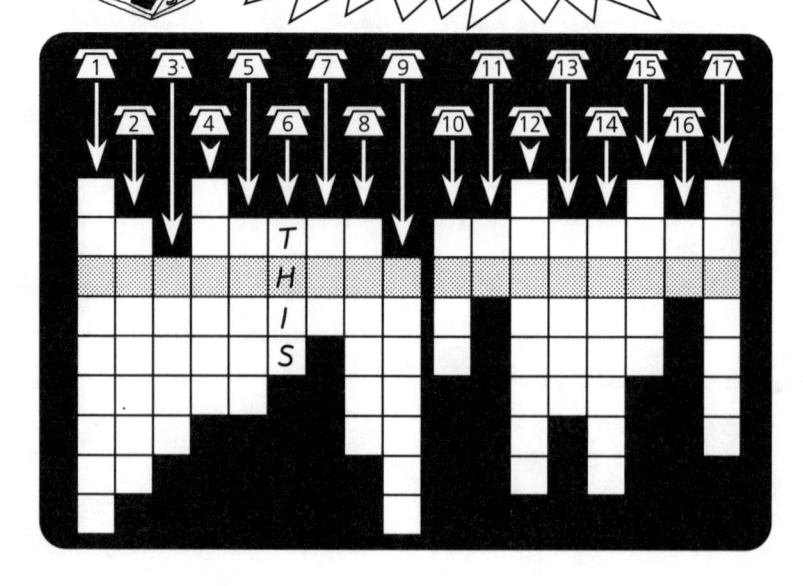

- [6] IS A VERY BAD LINE. COULD YOU SPEAK [11] A BIT?
- THE LINE'S [9]. I'LL TRY AGAIN LATER.
- IT'S RINGING, BUT THERE'S NO [8].
- COULD I SPEAK [16] SUSAN JONES, PLEASE?
- I THINK YOU HAVE THE [13] NUMBER.
- COULD I [5] TO DR. WATSON, PLEASE?
- [12].
- COULD I SPEAK TO MR. SMITH, [4]?
- I'LL PUT [7] THROUGH. WHO'S [14]?
- [1] 2582, PLEASE.
- PUTTING YOU [17].
- IF YOU'D LIKE TO [3] A [2], PLEASE SPEAK [15] THE [10].

PUZZLE 38  English Puzzles 4  Heinemann International

# Eight Special days

Each of the banners has the name of a special day written on it. (The small flags show if the day is special in the United Kingdom, the United States, or both.) Some of the letters are out of sight; these letters appear in the small boxes below the picture.

Take the letters from the banners and write them in the correct boxes, so that the names of the eight special days are complete.

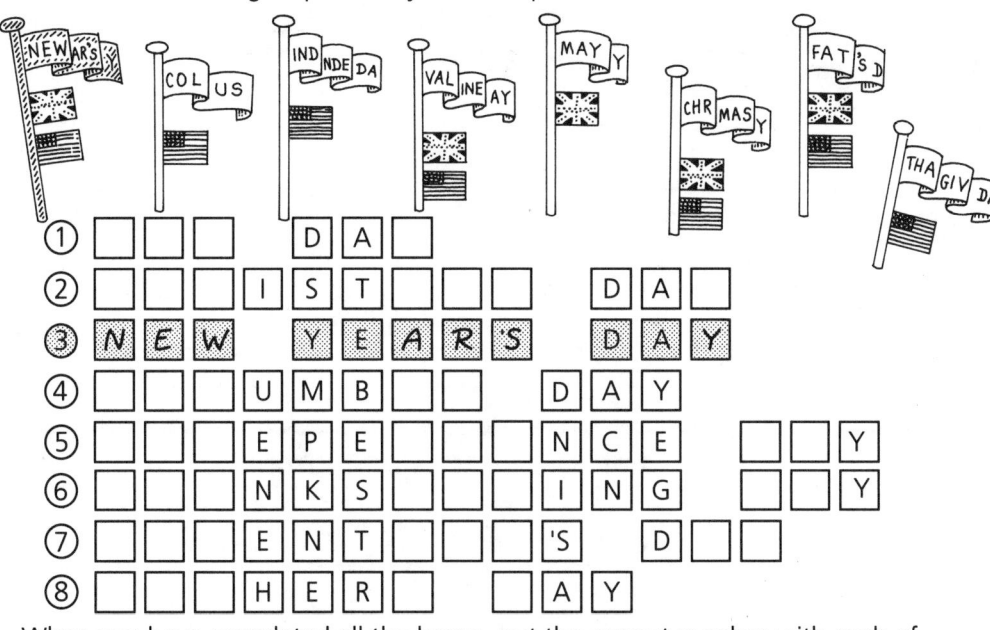

Banners: NEW ...AR'S, COL...US, IND...NDE...DA..., VAL...INE...AY, MAY...Y, CHR...MAS...Y, FAT...'S D..., THA...GIV...DA...

① ☐ ☐ ☐   D A ☐
② ☐ ☐ ☐ I S T ☐ ☐ ☐ D A ☐
③ N E W   Y E A R S   D A Y
④ ☐ ☐ ☐ U M B ☐ ☐ D A Y
⑤ ☐ ☐ ☐ E P E ☐ ☐ N C E   ☐ ☐ Y
⑥ ☐ ☐ ☐ N K S ☐ ☐ I N G   ☐ ☐ Y
⑦ ☐ ☐ ☐ E N T ☐ ☐ 'S   D ☐ ☐
⑧ ☐ ☐ ☐ H E R ☐   ☐ A Y

When you have completed all the boxes, put the correct number with each of these descriptions:

**A** The fourth Thursday in November – Day of giving thanks to God; often just called *Thanksgiving*.

**B** 14th February – Day on which people send romantic messages to each other.

**C** 1st May – Holiday in honour of workers.

**D** 1st January – The first day of the year.

**E** 12th October – Celebrates Christopher Columbus's arrival in the West Indies in 1492.

**F** The third Sunday in June – In honour of fathers.

**G** 25th December – Celebrates the birth of Jesus Christ.

**H** 4th July – Celebrates the American Declaration of Independence in 1776.

English Puzzles 4   Heinemann International

**PUZZLE 39**

# DICTIONARY DEFINITIONS

The American writer Ambrose Bierce (1842–1914) wrote a book called 'The Devil's Dictionary'. In this 'dictionary', he gave strange or amusing definitions of English words. Here are eight English words:

bore | defenceless | dentist | egotist | peace | reality | reconsider | year

First, put them with their *normal* definitions, and then put them with *Ambrose Bierce's* definitions.

## NORMAL DEFINITIONS

| # | word | definition |
|---|---|---|
| 1 | egotist | *n.* a person who believes that other people are not very important |
| 2 | | *n.* everything that is real |
| 3 | | *adj.* having no defence |
| 4 | | *n.* a period of twelve months |
| 5 | | *n.* an uninteresting person, especially a person who talks a lot in an uninteresting way |
| 6 | | *vb.* to think again about something |
| 7 | | *n.* the opposite of *war* |
| 8 | | *n.* a person who examines and treats teeth |

## AMBROSE BIERCE'S DEFINITIONS

| # | word | definition |
|---|---|---|
| 1 | | *n.* a person who talks when you wish* him to listen |
| 2 | | *n.* a period of three hundred and sixty-five disappointments |
| 3 | | *n.* a prestidigitator* who, putting metal in your mouth, pulls coins out of your pocket |
| 4 | | *n.* in international affairs, a period of cheating* between two periods of fighting |
| 5 | | *adj.* unable to attack |
| 6 | | *n.* the dream of a mad philosopher |
| 7 | egotist | *n.* a person of low of taste, more interested in himself than in me |
| 8 | | *vb.* to seek* a justification* for a decision already made |

*Help with some words in Ambrose Bierce's definitions:

wish = want
a prestidigitator = a magician
cheating = dishonesty
to seek = to look for
a justification = a good reason

Question:
What do the abbreviations *n.*, *adj.* and *vb.* mean?

PUZZLE 40            English Puzzles 4    Heinemann International

# Punctuation

First, complete the words for these twelve punctuation marks:

| . | F | U | L | L |   | S | T | O | P |   |   |
|---|---|---|---|---|---|---|---|---|---|---|---|
| , | C |   | M | M |   |   |   |   |   |   |   |
| : | S |   | M | - | C |   | L |   | N |   |   |
| ; |   | O | L |   | N |   |   |   |   |   |   |
| ' | A |   |   | S | T |   |   | P | H |   |   |
| ( ) | B |   |   | C | K | T | S |   |   |   |   |

| ' ' |   | Q U |   | T A T |   | N | M | R | S |
|---|---|---|---|---|---|---|---|---|---|
| ? | Q |   | E S T |   | N |   | A | K |   |
| ! | E X |   | A M |   | I | O | N |   | R K |
| - | H Y |   | H |   | N |   |   |   |   |
| — | D |   | H |   |   |   |   |   |   |
| ... | T H |   | E E |   | D | T |   |   |   |

Now read the jokes and famous remarks, and answer the questions.

## JOKES

**1**
A: Do you know it's costing me £950 to have my house painted?
B: Wouldn't it be cheaper just to have it photographed?

**2**
A: Why do you always answer a question with a question?
B: Why shouldn't I answer a question with a question?

**3**
A: How's your insomnia?
B: Worse – I can't even sleep when it's time to get up!

**4**
FAN: You were superb in 'Romeo and Juliet'.
ACTOR: I bet you say that to everyone who's superb.

**5**
TEACHER (in history class): Where was the American Declaration of Independence signed?
STUDENT: Er...At the bottom?

## FAMOUS REMARKS

**A**
California is a great place – if you're an orange.
FRED ALLEN
American comedian

**B**
In the future, everyone will be famous for fifteen minutes.
ANDY WARHOL   American artist

**C**
I wouldn't join any club that would have me as a member.
GROUCHO MARX
American comedian

**D**
If you have to ask what jazz is, you'll never know.
LOUIS ARMSTRONG
American musician

**E**
Flying on Concorde is great: it gives you three extra hours to find your luggage.
BOB HOPE
American comedian

## Questions:

| Which **joke** has: | |
|---|---|
| two colons, two full stops, a pair of quotation marks and an apostrophe? | 4 |
| two colons, two question marks, a pair of brackets and three dots? | |
| two colons, two question marks and an apostrophe? | |
| two colons, two question marks and two apostrophes? | |
| two colons, a question mark, a dash, an exclamation mark and three apostrophes? | |

| Which **famous remark** has: | |
|---|---|
| a full stop, a comma and an apostrophe? | |
| a full stop, a dash and an apostrophe? | |
| a full stop and a comma? | |
| a full stop and an apostrophe? | |
| a full stop and a colon? | |

English Puzzles 4   Heinemann International

# FOLDED TWICE

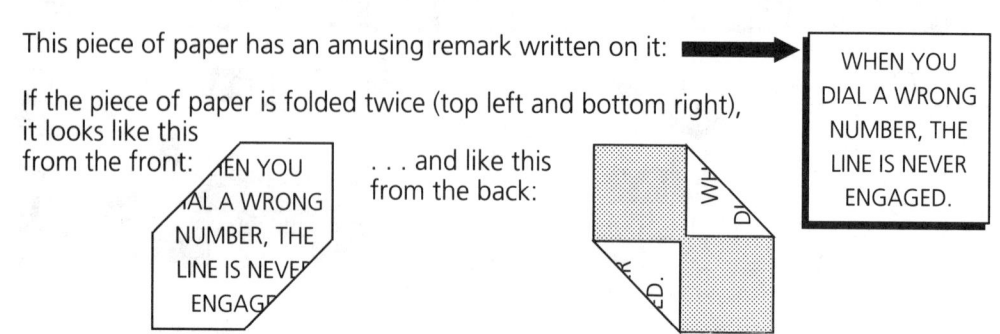

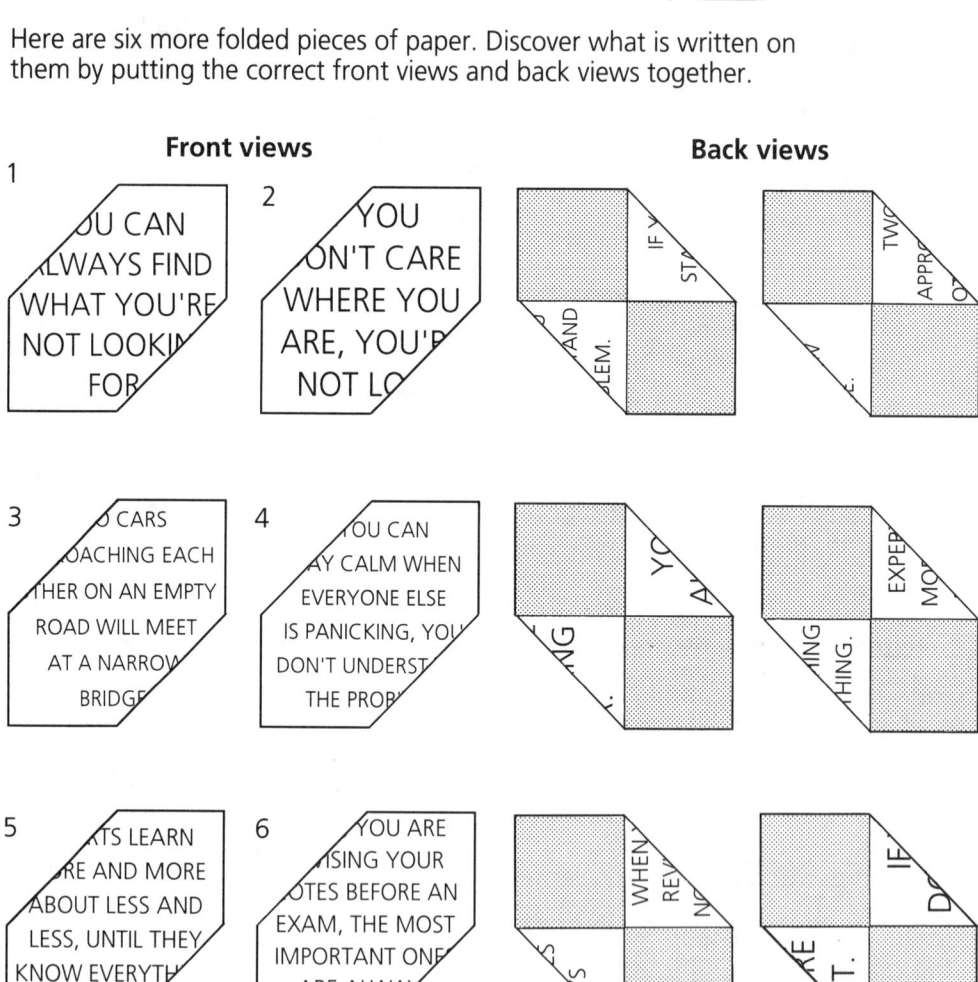

This piece of paper has an amusing remark written on it: ➡

> WHEN YOU DIAL A WRONG NUMBER, THE LINE IS NEVER ENGAGED.

If the piece of paper is folded twice (top left and bottom right), it looks like this from the front:

EN YOU
AL A WRONG
NUMBER, THE
LINE IS NEVE
ENGAG

... and like this from the back:

WH
D
ED.

Here are six more folded pieces of paper. Discover what is written on them by putting the correct front views and back views together.

**Front views**

1. U CAN
LWAYS FIND
WHAT YOU'RE
NOT LOOKI
FOR

2. YOU
ON'T CARE
WHERE YOU
ARE, YOU'R
NOT L

3. O CARS
OACHING EACH
HER ON AN EMPTY
ROAD WILL MEET
AT A NARROW
BRIDG

4. OU CAN
AY CALM WHEN
EVERYONE ELSE
IS PANICKING, YOU
DON'T UNDERST
THE PROB

5. TS LEARN
RE AND MORE
ABOUT LESS AND
LESS, UNTIL THEY
KNOW EVERYTH
ABOUT NO

6. YOU ARE
ISING YOUR
OTES BEFORE AN
EXAM, THE MOST
IMPORTANT ONE
ARE ALWA
ILLEGI

**Back views**

IF Y
ST
AND
LEM.

TWO
APPR
ING.
.

YO
NG
ING
HING.

EXPER
MO

WHEN
REV
N
TS
LE.

IF
D
RE
ST.

PUZZLE 42 English Puzzles 4 Heinemann International

# Close the shutters

This shutter [IF / PLAY / FIRE, / GET] has fallen off this window: ➡ [YOU / WITH / YOU / BURNT.]

When it is replaced, so that both shutters are closed, you can read an English proverb: ➡ [IF YOU / PLAY WITH / FIRE, YOU / GET BURNT.]

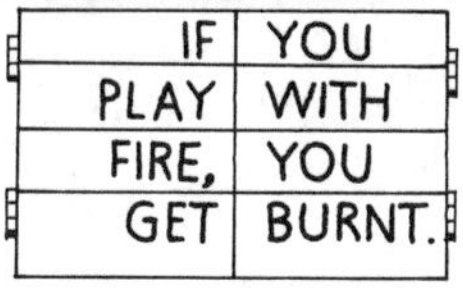

Replace the shutters on the eight windows below, so that you can read four more proverbs and the first lines of four songs.

① DON'T / MISTAKES, / DON'T / ANYTHING
Proverb

② YOU / SOMETHING / WELL, / YOURSELF.
Proverb

③ HAVE / LOVED, / HAVE / LIVED.
Proverb

④ JOB'S / DOING, / WORTH / WELL.
Proverb

⑤ HAD / HAMMER, / HAMMER / MORNING.
Trini Lopez 1963

⑥ FELL / WITH YOU, / PROMISE / TRUE?
The Beatles 1964

⑦ NEEDED / TO LOVE, / ONE THAT / THINKING OF.
The Hollies 1965

⑧ WERE A / AND YOU WERE / WOULD YOU / ANYWAY?
Tim Hardin 1966

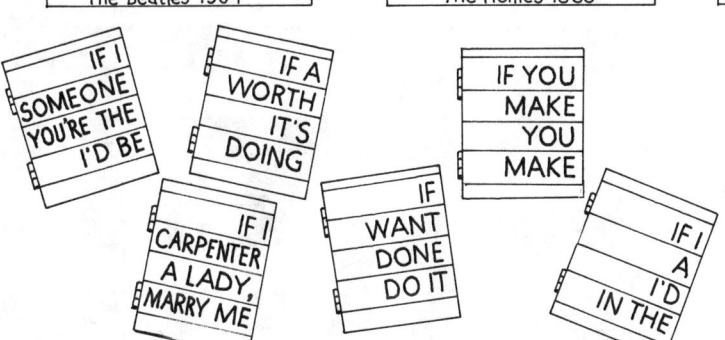

Loose shutters:
- IF I / SOMEONE / YOU'RE THE / I'D BE
- IF A / WORTH / IT'S / DOING
- IF YOU / MAKE / YOU / MAKE
- IF I / IN LOVE / WOULD YOU / TO BE
- IF I / CARPENTER / A LADY, / MARRY ME
- IF / WANT / DONE / DO IT
- IF I / A / I'D / IN THE
- IF YOU / NEVER / YOU / NEVER

| Question: | Numbers 1–4 are proverbs and 5–8 are the first lines of songs, but can you see *another* difference between 1–4 and 5–8? |

English Puzzles 4   Heinemann International

**PUZZLE** 43

# A COLLOQUIAL crossword

*Question:* What is the difference between *Yes* and *Yeah*?
*Answer:* They both have the same meaning, but *Yeah* is informal or 'colloquial'.

In this crossword, all the clues contain a colloquial word (in *italics*). For each one, find the word in the alphabetical list which has the same meaning, and write that word in the grid.

## Across

1. Has he got a lot of money?
   – Yeah, he's *loaded*!
6. If you don't go away, I'll call the *cops*.
9. Can you lend me ten *bucks*?
12. I've been *hard up* for years, but I've just got a good job so things should be better from now on.
13. What did you think of the film?
    – I thought it was *lousy*.
14. What do you think of George?
    – He's a really nice *guy*.
15. What was the restaurant like? – A bit *pricey*, but the food was very good.
16. Can you lend me ten *quid*?

## Down

2. They've got two *kids*: a boy and a girl.
3. Are you working tomorrow?
   – *Nope*.
4. Is there anything good on the *box* this evening?
5. Why are you looking at me like that? You think I'm *nuts*, don't you?
7. Do you like the Hurricanes?
   – Yeah, I think they're really *neat*.
8. How are you? – I'm a bit depressed. I've had a lot of *hassles* recently.
10. What did you think of the film?
    – It was interesting, but a bit *weird*.
11. Why did you do that? It was really *dumb*.

CHILDREN
DOLLARS
EXCELLENT
EXPENSIVE
MAD
MAN
NO
POLICE
POOR
POUNDS
PROBLEMS
(RICH)
STRANGE
STUPID
TELEVISION
TERRIBLE

PUZZLE 44    English Puzzles 4    Heinemann International

# DOUBLE MEANINGS

Quite a lot of English words have more than one meaning. Here are six examples:

| BANK | TANK | DATES | GLASSES | LETTERS | NAILS |

Put those words with the correct pairs of pictures.

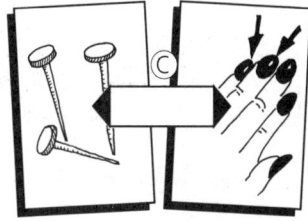

A. TANK
B. 
C. 
D. 
E. BANK
F. 

Use those six words to complete the answers to these six riddles.
(Use each word once.)

**1**
Q: Why is a postman's bag like the alphabet?
A: Because they're both full of .........

**2**
Q: Where do frogs keep their money?
A: In the river ...........

**3**
Q: Why should you always dry your hands carefully after washing them?
A: Because if you don't, your ..... will go rusty*.

**4**
Q: When a goldfish joins the army, where does it serve?
A: In the ......... division*.

**5**
Q: Why do history books taste good?
A: Because they're full of ........

**6**
Q: What should you give a short-sighted person* who likes drinking orange juice and milk at the same time?
A: A pair of ...........

* Help with some words in the riddles:

rusty = covered with rust (a red/brown substance which forms on metals)
division = part of an army
a short-sighted person = a person who cannot see things clearly when they are far away

English Puzzles 4   Heinemann International

# A very *emphatic* jigsaw

In each of these conversations, make the reply 'stronger' – more *emphatic* – by adding a word.
You can find the emphatic versions of the replies in the jigsaw. (The words of each reply are on pieces which are joined together.)

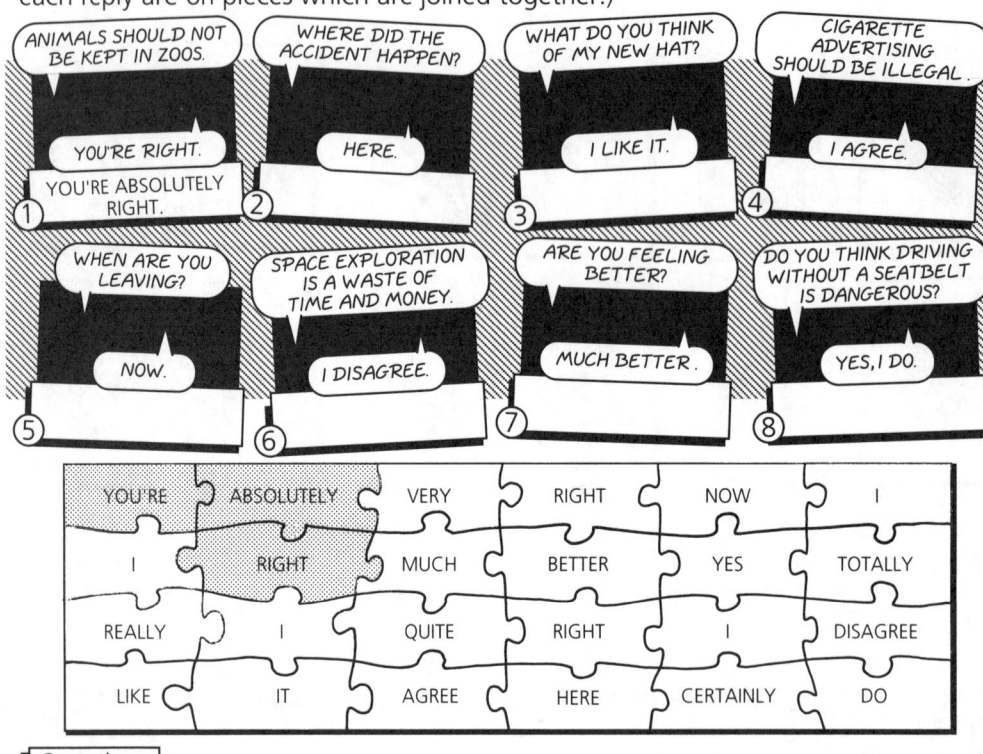

1. ANIMALS SHOULD NOT BE KEPT IN ZOOS. — YOU'RE RIGHT. / YOU'RE ABSOLUTELY RIGHT.
2. WHERE DID THE ACCIDENT HAPPEN? — HERE.
3. WHAT DO YOU THINK OF MY NEW HAT? — I LIKE IT.
4. CIGARETTE ADVERTISING SHOULD BE ILLEGAL. — I AGREE.
5. WHEN ARE YOU LEAVING? — NOW.
6. SPACE EXPLORATION IS A WASTE OF TIME AND MONEY. — I DISAGREE.
7. ARE YOU FEELING BETTER? — MUCH BETTER.
8. DO YOU THINK DRIVING WITHOUT A SEATBELT IS DANGEROUS? — YES, I DO.

Jigsaw pieces:

| YOU'RE | ABSOLUTELY | VERY | RIGHT | NOW | I |
| I | RIGHT | MUCH | BETTER | YES | TOTALLY |
| REALLY | I | QUITE | RIGHT | I | DISAGREE |
| LIKE | IT | AGREE | HERE | CERTAINLY | DO |

## Question:

Can you make the sentences below more emphatic by using these grey pieces to replace the grey pieces in the sentences?

NOT. | HUGE | EXHAUSTED. | AGES. | GREAT | CAN'T | STAND
DEFINITELY. | TINY | LOVE | DEFINITELY

(A) IT WAS A GOOD PARTY.
(B) I WAS BORN IN A SMALL VILLAGE.
(C) I'M TIRED.
(D) TOKYO IS A BIG CITY.
(E) YES.
(F) NO.
(G) I HAVEN'T SEEN YOU FOR A LONG TIME.
(H) I DON'T LIKE MODERN JAZZ.
(I) I'D LIKE TO VISIT PARIS.

PUZZLE 46 English Puzzles 4 Heinemann International

# MISPRINTS

In newspapers (and magazines, books, etc.), words are sometimes printed wrongly. Here are two examples:

| Ten musicians from the Bournemouth Sympathy Orchestra are to lose their jobs. | This word should be *Symphony*. |
|---|---|
| CLEANER REQUIRED, six hours per week, to clean small officers in Station Road, Witney. | This word should be *offices*. |

Mistakes like these are called 'misprints'. There are eight misprints in the texts below (one in each text). Can you find them and correct them?

**In each of these texts, the misprint is a wrong letter printed instead of the right letter.**

**In each of these texts, the misprint is a letter being omitted.**

**A** Never throw away old chicken bones. Put them in water and boil them with a few vegetables. This will make delicious soap.

→ soup

**E** The Prime Minister said today that the conference had been a hug success.

**B** Unless the teachers receive more pay, they may decide to leave their pests.

When you have corrected the misprints, you should be able to put the eight words from the boxes into this grid:

**F** Two men were taken to hospital suffering from buns.

**C** Before Miss Pollard concluded the concert, she was prevented with a bouquet of flowers by the mayor.

**G** John Mellor was found guilty of carless driving.

**D** The bride wore a white silk dress and carried a bouquet of punk flowers.

**H** The subject of the lecture will be 'Country life', and Mrs Walker will show photographs of some beautiful wild pants.

English Puzzles 4    Heinemann International

# Bits and pieces

Here are some English words which describe pieces of things:

BAR    BLOCK    CRUMB    DROP    GRAIN    LOAF
LUMP   PINCH    PLANK    SHEET   SLICE    SQUARE

Use those twelve words to do this puzzle. There are fifteen answers, so you will need to use some of the words more than once.

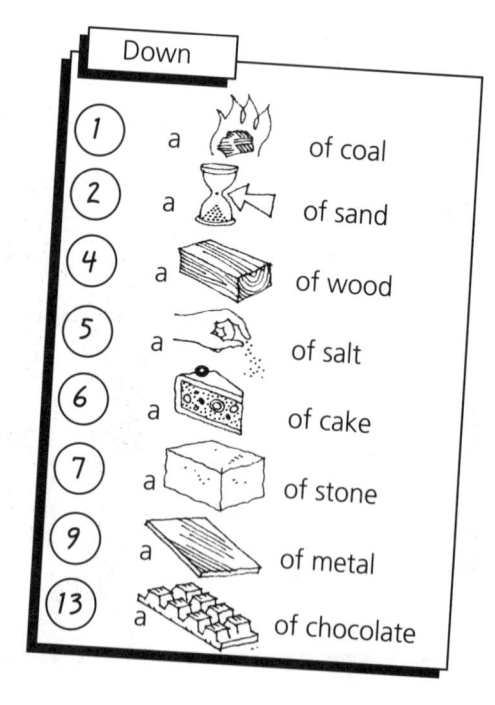

3 across: D R O P

## Across

3. a ___ of water
6. a ___ of bread
8. a ___ of wood
10. a ___ of bread
11. a ___ of paper
12. a ___ of bread
14. a ___ of chocolate

## Down

1. a ___ of coal
2. a ___ of sand
4. a ___ of wood
5. a ___ of salt
6. a ___ of cake
7. a ___ of stone
9. a ___ of metal
13. a ___ of chocolate

PUZZLE 48

English Puzzles 4   Heinemann International

# Contractions

Here are some contractions that you probably met very early in your English studies:

| 'm = am | 've = have | 's = is/has | 'd = had/would |

Here are some other contractions (you can meet them in informal or 'colloquial' texts, such as the words of pop songs):

—in' = —ing   *For example*: sittin' = sitting
'n' = and         'bout = about
'em = them      'cause = because

As usual, apostrophes represent missing letters – letters that are not pronounced. Write beside each of these song titles the letters represented by the apostrophes.

|  |  | | |
|---|---|---|---|
| ELVIS PRESLEY 1971 | I'M LEAVIN'. | A | G |
| THE COMMODORES 1986 | GOIN' TO THE BANK. | | |
| THE ROLLING STONES 1974 | IT'S ONLY ROCK'N'ROLL. | | |
| THIN LIZZY 1977 | DANCIN' IN THE MOONLIGHT. | | |
| CHILL FAC-TORR 1983 | TWIST (ROUND'N'ROUND). | | |
| PAUL McCARTNEY 1976 | LET 'EM IN. | | |
| BARBRA STREISAND 1982 | COMIN' IN AND OUT OF YOUR LIFE. | | |
| THE ROLLING STONES 1965 | TALKIN' 'BOUT YOU, BABY. | | |
| SILVER CONVENTION 1977 | EVERYBODY'S TALKIN' 'BOUT LOVE. | | |
| DIANA ROSS 1978 | LOVIN', LIVIN' AND GIVIN'. | | |
| HARRY NILSSON 1969 | EVERYBODY'S TALKIN'. | | |

Question:

If you have put all the letters in the correct squares, you should find the same word in both groups of *dark* squares. It is an informal or 'colloquial' word, often used by musicians. Do you know what it means?

English Puzzles 4   Heinemann International

# THE LAST WORD

Beside each of these verbs, write its Past Participle. You will need these Past Participles in the second part of the puzzle.

ACCOMPANY  ____    INCLUDE  ____

CARRY  ____    PERMIT  ____

EXAMINE  ____    REMOVE  ____

FORBID  ____    WEAR  ____

The last word is missing from each of the signs below. Complete the signs, using the Past Participles you have written above.

1. NO PARKING — ALL VEHICLES WILL BE ____

2. DOGS MUST BE ____

3. SERVICE IS ____

4. SMOKING IS STRICTLY ____

5. BUILDING WORK IN PROGRESS — HARD HATS MUST BE ____

6. THE BIG WHEEL — CHILDREN UNDER 12 MUST BE ____

7. AIRPORT — SECURITY CHECK — ALL BAGS WILL BE ____

8. THE TAKING OF PHOTOGRAPHS IS NOT ____

PUZZLE 50

# SOLUTIONS

## PUZZLE 1  Be careful!

1 REDUCE SPEED NOW
2 KEEP OFF THE GRASS
3 WET PAINT
4 LONG VEHICLE
5 DANGER
6 BEWARE OF THE DOG
7 CIGARETTES CAN SERIOUSLY DAMAGE YOUR HEALTH
8 NO SWIMMING WHEN THE RED FLAG IS FLYING
9 BEWARE OF PICKPOCKETS
10 MIND THE STEP

## PUZZLE 2  Geography and geometry

| V LAO | → | OVAL | 1 |
| IRL C EC | → | CIRCLE | 2 |
| E CO N | → | CONE | 3 |
| PE RH E S | → | SPHERE | 4 |
| DY IRL EC N | → | CYLINDER | 5 |
| GR IL ET N A | → | TRIANGLE | 6 |
| EC NL GR A ET | → | RECTANGLE | 7 |
| ET C R EC S N | → | CRESCENT | 8 |

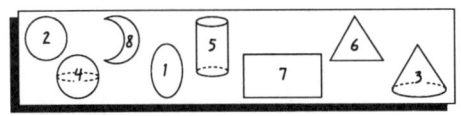

## PUZZLE 3  Twenty-one proverbs

1 Everything must have a beginning.
2 Something is better than nothing.
3 Nothing is certain except death and taxes.
4 Ask no questions and you'll hear no lies.
5 No news is good news.
6 Seeing is believing.
7 Don't cry before you're hurt.
8 Don't put all your eggs in one basket.
9 Love makes all hard hearts gentle.
10 All roads lead to Rome.
11 There are two sides to every question.
12 Time flies.
13 A friend to everybody is a friend to nobody.
14 All cats are grey in the dark.
15 You can't please everybody.
16 Every picture tells a story.
17 Money isn't everything.
18 It's a small world.
19 Money talks.
20 There's a time and a place for everything.
21 All good things must come to an end.

## PUZZLE 4  Bus queue

1 Have you been waiting long?
2 Do you think it's going to rain?
3 Would you like a piece of chocolate?
4 Are you tired?
5 Have you lost something?
6 Did you see the match on TV last night?
7 Are you having a holiday this year?
8 Have you seen any good films lately?
9 Do you need any help?

Note: Don't confuse *lately* with *late*. Lately means *recently*.

## PUZZLE 5  Find the key word

The key word is *love*.
NOUN – 2,4,8,9,14,19,20.
VERB: INFINITIVE – 3,5,12,18.
VERB: IMPERATIVE – 1,16,17.
VERB: PRESENT SIMPLE – 6,7,10,11,13,15.

Remember:
A lot of English words can be both nouns and verbs. *Love* is one example; here are some more: *answer, dream, drink, help, phone, plan, stop.*

## PUZZLE 6  Missing letters

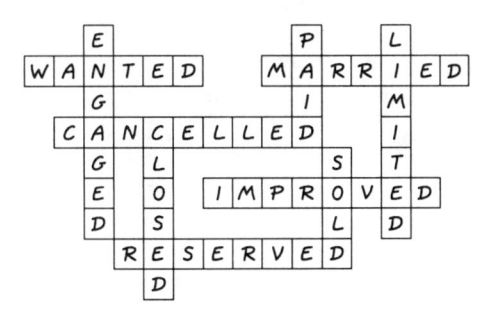

1 SOLD
2 RESERVED
3 WANTED
4 CLOSED
5 CANCELLED
6 PAID
7 ENGAGED
8 IMPROVED
9 MARRIED
10 LIMITED

## PUZZLE 7  Science ficton

Films from the 1970s:

THE CAT FROM OUTER SPACE
THE BLACK HOLE
BLACK MOON
THE DAY TIME ENDED
DIGBY, THE BIGGEST DOG IN THE WORLD

Films from the 1960s:

VOYAGE TO THE BOTTOM OF THE SEA
THE MAN WITH X-RAY EYES
THE LOST CONTINENT
THE DAY THE EARTH CAUGHT FIRE
IN THE YEAR 2889
THE TIME MACHINE

Films from the 1950s and the 1920s:

A MESSAGE FROM MARS
THE FLYING SAUCER
SATELLITE IN THE SKY
THE BEGINNING OF THE END
I MARRIED A MONSTER FROM OUTER SPACE
THE STORY WITHOUT A NAME
THE NIGHT THE WORLD EXPLODED

## PUZZLE 8  Exclamations!

1 MMM!
2 BOO!
3 WOW!
4 OUCH!
5 UGH!
6 HEY!
7 SHH!
8 BRR!
9 WHOOPS!
10 ATCHOO!
11 HA! HA!

Brr! I'm freezing!
Ouch! That hurt!
Boo! Rubbish!
Hey! Come back!
Ha! Ha! Very funny.
Shh! The baby's asleep.
Atchoo! I think I'm getting a cold.
Mmm! This is delicious!
Ugh! This tastes awful!
Whoops! Oh dear, it's broken.
Wow! That's fantastic!

Answer to question:
These are the pronunciations: *Mmm!*/ əm /, *Boo!*/ buː /, *Wow!*/ waʊ /, *Ouch!*/ aʊtʃ /, *Ugh!*/ ɜː /, *Hey!*/ heɪ /, *Shh!*/ ʃ /, *Brr!*/ bɜːr /, *Whoops!*/ wʊps /, *Atchoo!*/ æˈtʃuː /, *Ha! Ha!*/ hɑːhɑː /.

## PUZZLE 9  Imaginary jobs and real jobs

1 opera singer
2 lorry driver
3 hotel manager
4 newspaper editor
5 wedding photographer
6 aircraft technician
7 driving instructor
8 ballet dancer
9 rock musician
10 construction worker
11 computer programmer
12 film director

## PUZZLE 10  Pairs of words

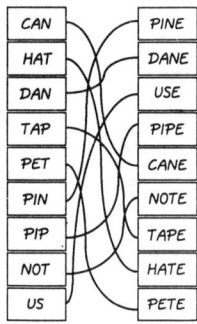

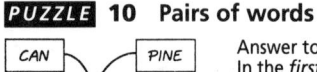

| CAN | PINE |
| HAT | DANE |
| DAN | USE |
| TAP | PIPE |
| PET | CANE |
| PIN | NOTE |
| PIP | TAPE |
| NOT | HATE |
| US  | PETE |

Answer to question:
In the *first* word in each pair (CAN, HAT, DAN, TAP, PET, etc.), the vowel is 'short':
a = / æ /, e = / e /,
i = / ɪ /, o = / ɒ /,
u = / ʌ /.
In the *second* word in each pair (CANE, HATE, DANE, TAPE, PETE, etc.), the vowel is 'long':
a = / eɪ /, e = / iː /,
i = / aɪ /, o = / əʊ /,
u = / juː /.

## PUZZLE 11  Abbreviations

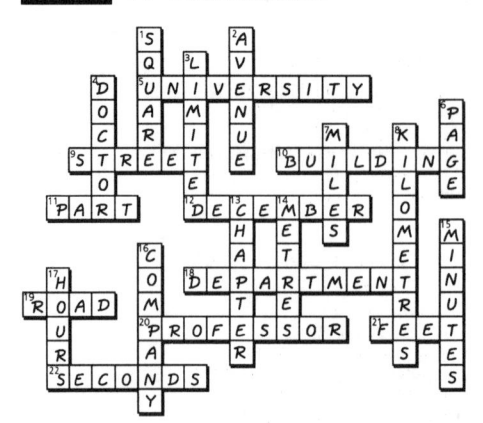

Crossword:
Across: UNIVERSITY, STREET, BUILDING, PART, DECEMBER, ROAD, DEPARTMENT, PROFESSOR, FEET, SECONDS
Down: SQUARE, AVENUE, DOCTOR, DRIVE, MINUTE, MOUNT, KILOMETRES, PAGE, HEIGHT, COMPANY, MONSIEUR, YARDS

## PUZZLE 12  A strange quiz

1 They get wet.
2 Because umbrellas can't walk.
3 A very wet one.
4 Because it wasn't raining.
5 To keep his trousers up.
6 The soldier with the biggest feet.
7 Holes.
8 A shadow.
9 Stop paying your water bill.
10 The kind that makes its own wine.
11 To join their heads to their bodies.
12 Because there are more of them.

## PUZZLE 13  A very official jigsaw

1 What is your occupation?
2 What is your marital status?
3 What is your age?
4 What is your height?*
5 What is your weight? *
6 What is your country of residence?
7 What is your full postal address?

* Remember: Although their spelling is similar, the words *height* / haɪt / and *weight* / weɪt / do not rhyme.

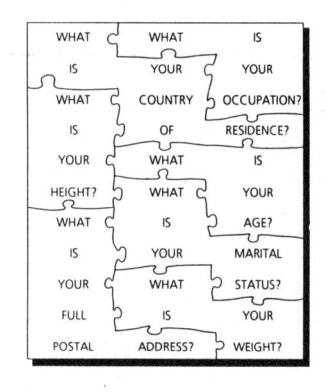

## PUZZLE 14  Grammar files

1 ADJECTIVES
2 ADJECTIVES (POSSESSIVE)
3 ADVERBS
4 ARTICLE (DEFINITE)
5 ARTICLE (INDEFINITE)
6 CONJUNCTIONS
7 NOUNS (UNCOUNTABLE)
8 NOUNS (COUNTABLE, SINGULAR)
9 NOUNS (COUNTABLE, PLURAL)
10 PREPOSITIONS
11 PRONOUNS (SUBJECT)
12 PRONOUNS (OBJECT)
13 PRONOUNS (POSSESSIVE)
14 VERBS (REGULAR): INFINITIVE
15 VERBS (IRREGULAR): INFINITIVE
16 VERBS: -ing FORM
17 VERBS: PAST SIMPLE FORM
18 VERBS: PAST PARTICIPLE

## PUZZLE 15 Documents for the files

A:2  D:8   G:17  J:18  P:4
B:6  E:15  H:3   K:10  N:7   Q:12
C:11 F:5   I:13  L:9   O:1   R:16

Answer to question:
In the documents which don't have (*etc.*) at the end, the lists of words are *complete*. Document A shows all the Possessive Adjectives; document C shows all the Subject Pronouns; document F shows the two forms of the Indefinite Article; document I shows all the Possessive Pronouns; document P shows the only form of the Definite Article, and document Q shows all the Object Pronouns.

In the documents which have (*etc.*) at the end, the lists of words are just *examples*. For instance, document B shows four conjunctions, but there are others.

## PUZZLE 16 Strong feelings

1  A) surprised    B) astonished
2  A) worried      B) desperate
3  A) interested   B) fascinated
4  A) pleased      B) delighted
5  A) shocked      B) horrified
6  A) excited      B) thrilled

## PUZZLE 17 Telegram language

3 A newspaper headline.
    The Prime Minister has been admitted to hospital.
7 A sentence from a recipe.
    Wash the apples in warm water and cut them into quarters.
2 A sentence from a diary.
    I wanted to go to the beach, but the weather was terrible.
4 Three sentences from a postcard.
    We're having a great holiday. The weather is marvellous. We'll see you in two weeks.
6 A proverb.
    If you have cold hands, you have a warm heart.
1 A message.
    I've gone to lunch. I'll be back at 2.15.
5 Another message.
    I need to speak to you urgently. I'll be at home all evening. Please phone me.

Note: The proverb is always said in its 'telegram language' form, *Cold hands, warm heart.*

## PUZZLE 18 Logical laws

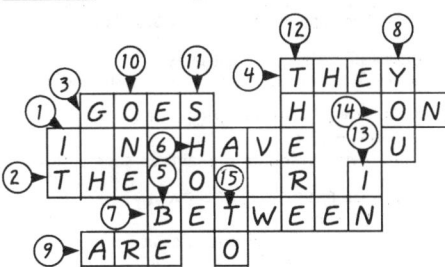

(crossword grid with answers: GOES, THEY, ON, IN, HAVE, THE, SO, R, I, U, BETWEEN, ARE, O)

## PUZZLE 19 At the theatre

The ten words are:
1 THE  2 OLD  3 COUNTRY  4 DAY  5 SUMMER
6 AND  7 SONS  8 ALL  9 I  10 NIGHT
So the titles of the plays are:
THE OLD COUNTRY
ONE FINE DAY
SUMMER
FATHERS AND SONS
THE LONG, THE SHORT AND THE TALL
ALL MY SONS
THE MAN WHO HAD ALL THE LUCK
ANOTHER COUNTRY
TILL THE DAY I DIE
NIGHT SCHOOL
OLD TIMES
A NIGHT OUT
I HAVE BEEN HERE BEFORE
NIGHT AND DAY
MOTHER'S DAY
SUDDENLY LAST SUMMER

## PUZZLE 20 Disc jockey

1 *love*, 2 *love*, 3 *love*, 4 *loved*, 5 *loving*,
6 *loved*, 7 *loving*, 8 *love*, 9 *love*, 10 *loving*,
11 *love*, 12 *loved*.

Answers to questions:
1 ①③⑪   2 ④⑫   3 ⑥   4 ⑩

## PUZZLE 21 House and garden

1 Chimney        8 Fence
2 TV aerial      9 Gate
3 Roof          10 Path
4 Satellite dish 11 Letterbox
5 Balcony       12 Shutter
6 Doorbell      13 Porch
7 Steps         14 Burglar alarm

## PUZZLE 22 What do they really mean?

1 Roundabout              9 Picnic area
2 Hump ahead             10 Museum
3 Road works ahead       11 Camping site
4 Quayside or river bank 12 Information
5 Low-flying aircraft    13 Parking area
6 No U-turns             14 Hospital
7 No right turn          15 Road narrows on
8 No motor vehicles         both sides

## PUZZLE 23 Interesting facts

20, 80, 10, 3, 200, 4, 5, 5, 50, 7, 9, 27, 50, 30, TOTAL: 500
A woodpecker can peck *five hundred* times per minute.

## PUZZLE 24 Folded paper

1 *TOO MANY GAMES*      5 *HALF A MINUTE*
2 *TOO MUCH TROUBLE*    6 *ONE MORE SATURDAY*
3 *ONE OF US*              *NIGHT*
4 *MOST OF US ARE SAD*  7 *NO MORE LONELY NIGHTS*

A *ONE OF OUR AIRCRAFT IS MISSING*
B *ONE MORE RIVER*
C *ONE IN A MILLION*
D *ONE BY ONE*

## PUZZLE 25 What are they saying?

A How long have you been studying Chinese?
B It's been raining all morning.
C We've been looking forward to this holiday for months.
D It's been doing that all morning.
E I haven't been feeling very well recently, doctor.
F How long have you been working on it?
G Have you been waiting long?
H You've been working too hard.

The tense is the *Present Perfect Continuous*. This tense is used in all the sentences in the pictures.

## PUZZLE 26 The second half

RICH MAN, POOR MAN — Irwin Shaw
BLUE EYES, BLACK HAIR — Marguerite Duras
BLACK FACES, WHITE FACES — Jane Gardam
INSIDE, OUTSIDE — Herman Wouk
I'M O.K., YOU'RE O.K. — Thomas A. Harris
DARK GREEN, BRIGHT RED — Gore Vidal
A LITTLE TEA, A LITTLE CHAT — Christina Stead
GOOD TIMES, BAD TIMES — Harold Evans
OTHER VOICES, OTHER ROOMS — Truman Capote

Answers to questions:
(A) The book about psychology is *I'm O.K., You're O.K.*
(B) The autobiography is *Good Times, Bad Times*.

## PUZZLE 27 Grammatical terms

A SENTENCES
B SUFFIXES
C SYLLABLES
D PHRASES
E CONSONANTS
F VOWELS
G LETTERS
H WORDS
I PREFIXES

1 In this *phrase*, there are three *words*.
2 This *word* has nine *letters*.
3 This *word* has a *prefix* and a *suffix*.
4 This *word* has only one *syllable*.
5 In this *sentence*, there are four *words*.
6 In this *word*, there are four *vowels* and six *consonants*.

## PUZZLE 28 Shopping list

1 INK
2 WRITING PAPER
3 MATCHES
4 JAM
5 ORANGE JUICE
6 TOOTHPASTE
7 SARDINES
8 SELLOTAPE
9 CHOCOLATE
10 BISCUITS

SHOPPING LIST
a packet of biscuits
a tube of toothpaste
a tin of sardines
a bottle of ink
a jar of jam
a box of matches
a carton of orange juice
a bar of chocolate
a roll of sellotape
a pad of writing paper

## PUZZLE 29 More logical laws

A:9  B:3  C:1  D:7  E:8
F:4  G:10  H:6  I:5  J:2

## PUZZLE 30 A very polite jigsaw

1 Please take a seat.
2 I don't really like spaghetti.
3 Just a moment, please.
4 I'd love to but I can't.
5 I'd rather you didn't.
6 I'm afraid not.
7 I don't mind.
8 Not really.
9 I'm afraid he's out.

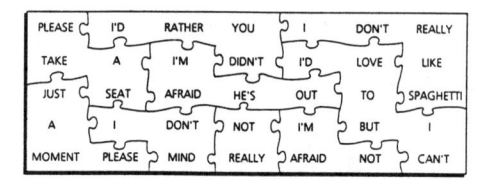

## PUZZLE 31 Titles and authors

1 A HOT DAY IN SUMMER by I. Scream.
  (*I. Scream* sounds the same as 'ice-cream'.)

2 THE SOUTH POLE by Anne Tarktik.
  (*Anne Tarktik* sounds the same as 'Antarctic'.)

3 HORROR STORIES by R.U. Frightened.
  (*R.U. Frightened* sounds the same as 'Are you frightened?')

4 ON THE BEACH by C. Shorr.
  (*C. Shorr* sounds the same as 'sea shore'.)

5 THE JUDGE HAS JUST COME IN by Stan Dupp.
  (*Stan Dupp* sounds the same as 'Stand up'.)

6 DON'T BE LATE! by Justin Tyme.
  (*Justin Tyme* sounds the same as 'just in time'.)

7 DO BLACK CATS BRING GOOD LUCK? by Sue Perstishen.
  (*Sue Perstishen* sounds the same as 'superstition'.)

8 THERE'S A PARTY ON SATURDAY by Will U.B.There.
  (*Will U.B.There* sounds the same as 'Will you be there?'.)

## PUZZLE 32  Typing mistakes

```
                                    75 North Square
                                    Clifdon CL31 7PR
The Royal Hotel                     November 25th 1991
Church Road
Hillborough HI25 7RJ

Dear Sir/Madam
Please reserve in my name a single room with
bath/shower for the night of Wednesday December
18th.
Please also let me know whether you allow dogs
in the hotel, as mine will probably be travelling
with me.
Yours faithfully
John Smith
John Smith
```

```
              THE ROYAL HOTEL
          CHURCH ROAD  HILLBOROUGH  HI25 7RJ

Mr John Smith                       November 27th 1991
75 North Square
Clifdon CL31 7PR

Dear Mr Smith
Thank you for your letter of November 25th.
I have been a hotel manager for forty years, and
have never had any problems with dogs.
- Dogs have never fallen asleep with cigarettes in
  in their hands and burnt their beds.
- Dogs have never stolen towels from their rooms.
- Dogs have never paid their bills with bad cheques.
Your dog will be welcome.
Yours sincerely
J.T.Brown
J.T.Brown
Manager
P.S. If your dog promises that you will not cause
any problems, you will be welcome too.
```

## PUZZLE 33  The World Cup

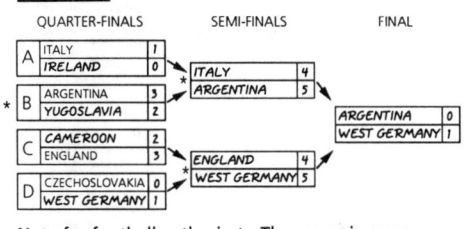

```
QUARTER-FINALS      SEMI-FINALS         FINAL

A  ITALY      1
   IRELAND    0   *  ITALY      4
                     ARGENTINA  5
*B ARGENTINA  3
   YUGOSLAVIA 2                    ARGENTINA    0
                                   WEST GERMANY 1
C  CAMEROON   2
   ENGLAND    3      ENGLAND      4
                  *  WEST GERMANY 5
D  CZECHOSLOVAKIA 0
   WEST GERMANY   1
```

Note for football enthusiasts: The scores in some matches (those marked *) included penalties after extra time.

## PUZZLE 34  Hotel rooms

A  Do you have a single room for tonight?
B  What's the price per night?
C  Is breakfast included?
D  Can I have breakfast in my room?
E  I'm checking out tomorrow.*
F  Could you have my bill ready?
G  There's a mistake in my bill.
H  I didn't make any phone calls.

*Remember: When you leave a hotel, you check out; when you arrive at a hotel, you check in.

Note: When you say room numbers such as 101, 206, etc., say the figures individually, and say the figure 0 like the letter O: 101 is ONE-O-ONE, 206 is TWO-O-SIX, etc.

## PUZZLE 35  Bricks in a wall

1  *I'M OFF*. BYE!
2  HELLO, EVERYONE. *I'M BACK*.
3  YOU DON'T LOOK VERY HAPPY. *WHAT'S UP*?
4  *HE'S OUT*. BUT HE'S COMING BACK LATER TODAY.
5  LET'S GO TO THE CINEMA. – O.K. *WHAT'S ON*?
6  *HE'S IN*. BUT HE DOESN'T WANT TO BE DISTURBED.
7  *HE'S AWAY*. HE'S NOT COMING BACK UNTIL
   THE END OF THE MONTH.

Remember the difference between *He's out* (He's absent, but not far away and possibly not for very long) and *He's away* (He's absent, possibly quite far away and for quite a long time).
Remember also: *I'm off* means *I'm leaving*; *What's up?* means *What's the matter?/ What's wrong?*; *What's on (at the cinema)?* means *What film can we see?*

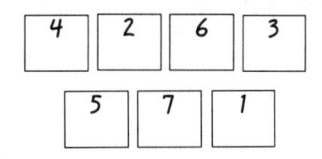

| 4 | 2 | 6 | 3 |
|---|---|---|---|
| 5 | 7 | 1 |   |

Answers to questions:
*I'm down* means *I'm unhappy*.
*It's over* means *It's finished*.

## PUZZLE 36  A phonetic crossword

| British Airways | 11 Down |
| British Broadcasting Corporation | 11 Across |
| British Rail | 2 Down |
| Central Intelligence Agency | 12 Down |
| European Community | 5 Down |
| Federal Bureau of Investigation | 7 Down |
| Great Britain | 1 Across |
| Los Angeles | 3 Down |
| Member of Parliament | 8 Across |
| Organization of African Unity | 15 Across |
| Please turn over | 9 Down |
| Royal Air Force | 6 Across |
| Please reply (*from the French: Répondez s'il vous plaît*) | 17 Across |
| Science Fiction | 14 Across |
| Unidentified Flying Object | 13 Down |
| United Nations | 16 Down |
| United States of America | 13 Across |
| Union of Soviet Socialist Republics | 10 Down |
| Very important person | 4 Across |

## PUZZLE 37  Knock! Knock!

1  Ken. (*Ken* I come in?/*Can* I come in?)
2  Harry. (*Harry* up and open the door!/ *Hurry* up and open the door!)
3  Mary. (*Mary* Christmas!/ *Merry* Christmas!)
4  Howard. (*Howard* I know?/ *How would* I know?)
5  Paul. (*Paul* harder and maybe the door will open./ *Pull* harder and maybe the door will open.)
6  Betty. (*Betty* late than never!/ *Better* late than never!)

## PUZZLE 38 On the telephone

The job which appears in the special squares is *telephone operator*.

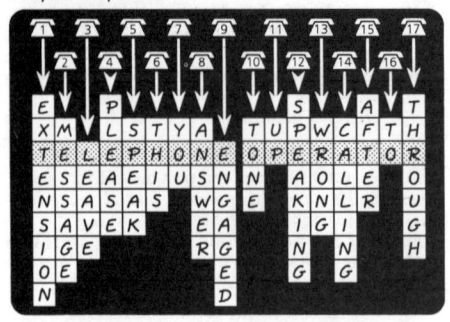

```
   1   3   5   7   9   11  13  15  17
   ↓   ↓   ↓   ↓   ↓   ↓   ↓   ↓   ↓
     2   4   6   8   10  12  14  16
     ↓   ↓   ↓   ↓   ↓   ↓   ↓   ↓
   E   P           S       A   T
 X M L S T Y A   T U P W C F T H
 T E L E P H O N E   O P E R A T O R
 E S E A E I U S N   N A O L E O
 N S A S A S   W G E   K N L R   U
 S A V E K     E A     I G I     G
 I   G E       R G     N N       H
 O   E         E       N G
 N                     D
```

Note: 'The line's *engaged*' is British English; the American English equivalent is 'The line's *busy*'.

## PUZZLE 39 Eight special days

1 MAY DAY
2 CHRISTMAS DAY
3 NEW YEAR'S DAY
4 COLUMBUS DAY
5 INDEPENDENCE DAY
6 THANKSGIVING DAY
7 VALENTINE'S DAY
8 FATHER'S DAY*

A:6, B:7, C:1, D:3, E:4, F:8, G:2, H:5.

*Note: *Mother's Day* is the second Sunday in May in the US, and the fourth Sunday in Lent (the period before Easter) in the UK.

## PUZZLE 40 Dictionary definitions

| NORMAL DEFINITIONS | AMBROSE BIERCE'S DEFINITIONS |
|---|---|
| 1 egotist | 1 bore |
| 2 reality | 2 year |
| 3 defenceless | 3 dentist |
| 4 year | 4 peace |
| 5 bore | 5 defenceless |
| 6 reconsider | 6 reality |
| 7 peace | 7 egotist |
| 8 dentist | 8 reconsider |

Answer to question:
The abbreviations *n.*, *adj.* and *vb.* mean *noun*, *adjective* and *verb*.

## PUZZLE 41 Punctuation

```
. F U L L   S T O P
, C O M M A
; S E M I - C O L O N
: C O L O N
' A P O S T R O P H E
( ) B R A C K E T S
" Q U O T A T I O N   M A R K S
? Q U E S T I O N   M A R K
! E X C L A M A T I O N   M A R K
- H Y P H E N
— D A S H
... T H R E E   D O T S
```

Answers to questions:
About the jokes
4; 5; 2; 1; 3.
About the famous remarks
D; A; B; C; E.

Note: In American English, a *full stop* is called a *period*.

## PUZZLE 42 Folded twice

1. YOU CAN ALWAYS FIND WHAT YOU'RE NOT LOOKING FOR.

2. IF YOU DON'T CARE WHERE YOU ARE, YOU'RE NOT LOST.

3. TWO CARS APPROACHING EACH OTHER ON AN EMPTY ROAD WILL MEET AT A NARROW BRIDGE.

4. IF YOU CAN STAY CALM WHEN EVERYONE ELSE IS PANICKING, YOU DON'T UNDERSTAND THE PROBLEM.

5. EXPERTS LEARN MORE AND MORE ABOUT LESS AND LESS, UNTIL THEY KNOW EVERYTHING ABOUT NOTHING.

6. WHEN YOU ARE REVISING YOUR NOTES BEFORE AN EXAM, THE MOST IMPORTANT ONES ARE ALWAYS ILLEGIBLE.

## PUZZLE 43 Close the shutters

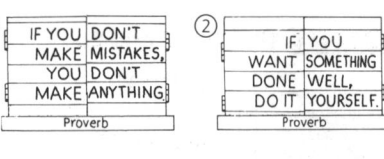

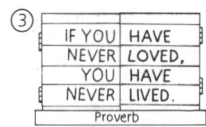

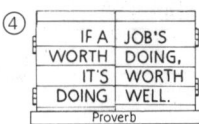

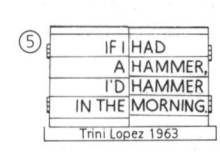

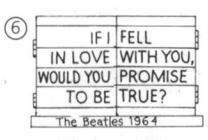

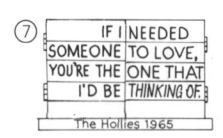

1. IF YOU DON'T MAKE MISTAKES, YOU DON'T MAKE ANYTHING.
   Proverb

2. IF YOU WANT SOMETHING DONE WELL, DO IT YOURSELF.
   Proverb

3. IF YOU HAVE NEVER LOVED, YOU HAVE NEVER LIVED.
   Proverb

4. IF A JOB'S WORTH DOING, IT'S WORTH DOING WELL.
   Proverb

5. IF I HAD A HAMMER, I'D HAMMER IN THE MORNING.
   Trini Lopez 1963

6. IF I FELL IN LOVE WITH YOU, WOULD YOU PROMISE TO BE TRUE?
   The Beatles 1964

7. IF I NEEDED SOMEONE TO LOVE, YOU'RE THE ONE THAT I'D BE THINKING OF.
   The Hollies 1965

8. IF I WERE A CARPENTER AND YOU WERE A LADY, WOULD YOU MARRY ME ANYWAY?
   Tim Hardin 1966

Answer to question:
In Numbers 1–4, the word *if* is followed by a verb in a *present* tense (*Present Simple* in 1, 2 and 4; *Present Perfect* in 3).
In Numbers 5–8, the word *if* is followed by a verb in a *past* tense (*Past Simple* in all four).

## PUZZLE 44 A colloquial crossword

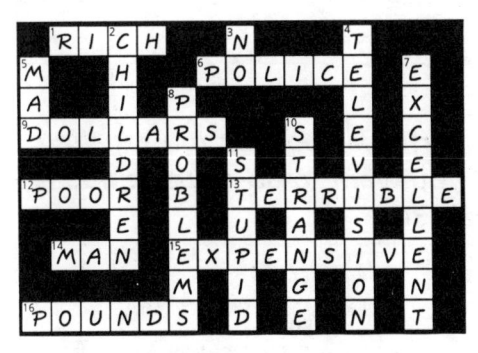

```
 R I C H . . N . . T . .
M . H . . P O L I C E .
A . I . P . . . L . X .
D O L L A R S . S E C .
 . . D . . . S T V . E .
P O O R . B T E R R I B L E
 . . E . L . U . A . . L
M A N . E X P E N S I V E
 . . . . M . I . O . . .
P O U N D S . D . N . T .
```

Note: The colloquial words *quid* ( = pound/pounds), *pricey* ( = expensive) and *the box* ( = the TV) are British English; *buck* ( = dollar), *neat* ( = excellent) and *dumb* ( = stupid) are American English. All the others are used in both British English and American English.

## PUZZLE 45 Double meanings

A: TANK    C: NAILS    E: BANK
B: GLASSES D: DATES    F: LETTERS

1 Because they're both full of *letters*.
2 In the river *bank*.
3 Because if you don't, your *nails* will go rusty.
4 In the *tank* division.
5 Because they're full of *dates*.
6 A pair of *glasses*.

## PUZZLE 46 A very emphatic jigsaw

1 You're absolutely right.   5 Right now.
2 Right here.                6 I totally disagree.*
3 I really like it.          7 Very much better.
4 I quite agree.*            8 Yes, I certainly do.

*Note: It is possible to say *I totally agree* instead of *I quite agree*, but it is not possible to say *I quite disagree* instead of *I totally disagree*.

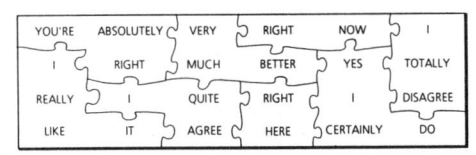

| YOU'RE | ABSOLUTELY | VERY | RIGHT | NOW | I |
| I | RIGHT | MUCH | BETTER | YES | TOTALLY |
| REALLY | I | QUITE | RIGHT | I | DISAGREE |
| LIKE | IT | AGREE | HERE | CERTAINLY | DO |

A It was a *great* party.
B I was born in a *tiny* village.
C I'm *exhausted*.
D Tokyo is a *huge* city.
E *Definitely*.
F *Definitely* not.
G I haven't seen you for *ages*.
H I *can't stand* modern jazz.
I I'd *love* to visit Paris.

## PUZZLE 47 Misprints

A: soap ← soup
B: pests ← posts
C: prevented ← presented
D: punk ← pink
E: hug ← huge
F: buns ← burns
G: carless ← careless
H: pants ← plants

```
       B   P I N K
       U   L
     C A   A
     A N   T
   P R E S E N T E D
     E   E
     L   P O S T S
     E   H
     S O U P
       G
       E
```

## PUZZLE 48 Bits and pieces

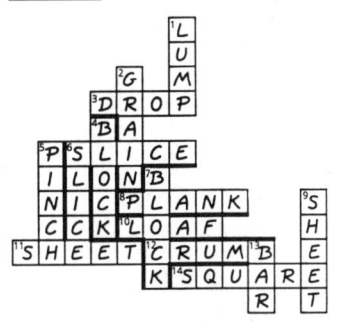

```
        L
        U
      G M
     D R O P
     B A
   P S L I C E
   I L O N B
   N I C P L A N K
   C C K L O A F     S
  S H E E T C R U M B E
         K S Q U A R E
              R     T
```

The words used more than once are:
– *block* (a block of wood, a block of stone),
– *sheet* (a sheet of paper, a sheet of metal),
– *slice* (a slice of bread, a slice of cake).

## PUZZLE 49 Contractions

| | |
|---|---|
| I'M LEAVIN'. | A G |
| GOIN' TO THE BANK. | **G** |
| IT'S ONLY ROCK'N'ROLL. | **I** A D |
| DANCIN' IN THE MOONLIGHT. | **G** |
| TWIST (ROUND'N'ROUND). | A D |
| LET 'EM IN. | T H |
| COMIN' IN AND OUT OF YOUR LIFE. | G |
| TALKIN' 'BOUT YOU, BABY. | **G** A |
| EVERYBODY'S TALKIN' 'BOUT LOVE. | **I** G A |
| LOVIN', LIVIN' AND GIVIN'. | **G** G G |
| EVERYBODY'S TALKIN'. | I G |

Answer to question:
A *gig* is a 'concert' or a 'performance' (of rock music or jazz): *It was a good gig – I really enjoyed it; We have a gig tomorrow night in Oxford*, etc.

## PUZZLE 50 The last word

1 NO PARKING – ALL VEHICLES WILL BE REMOVED
2 DOGS MUST BE CARRIED
3 SERVICE IS INCLUDED
4 SMOKING IS STRICTLY FORBIDDEN
5 BUILDING WORK IN PROGRESS – HARD HATS MUST BE WORN
6 THE BIG WHEEL – CHILDREN UNDER 12 MUST BE ACCOMPANIED
7 SECURITY CHECK – ALL BAGS WILL BE EXAMINED
8 THE TAKING OF PHOTOGRAPHS IS NOT PERMITTED

# Index

*If you want to do puzzles about particular points, you can find them in this Index. For example, if you want to do a puzzle about abbreviations, do Puzzle 11 or Puzzle 36.*

Abbreviations **11, 36**
Adjectives (about feelings) **16**
Adverbial particles **35**
*after/before/as soon as*, etc. **29**
*all/no/every*, etc. **3**
Alphabet, pronunciation of **36**
Apostrophe **49**
Books **26, 31**
Building, parts of **21**
Colloquial expressions **44, 49**
Compound nouns **9**
Conditional sentences **18, 43**
Conjunctions of time **29**
Containers **28**
Contractions **49**
Countries **2, 33**
Definitions **40**
*-ed* ending (verbs) **20**
Ellipsis **4, 17**
Emotions **16**
Emphasis **46**
*every/everything*, etc. **3**
Exclamations **8**
Films **7, 24**
Football **33**
Grammatical terms **14, 15, 19, 27**
Homonyms **45**
Hotels **32, 34**
*if*-clauses **18, 43**
Imperative/Infinitive **5**
*in/out/up/down*, etc. **35**
*-ing* ending (verbs) **20, 49**
Jobs **9**
Jokes **31, 37, 41**
Letters, formal **32**
Logical laws **18, 29, 42**
*most of/one more*, etc. **24**
*no/nothing*, etc. **3**
Nouns
– compound **9**
– the same as verbs **5**
– with two meanings **45**
Numerical expressions **23**

Official style **13**
Omission of words **4, 17**
Passive **50**
Past participles **6, 50**
Past Simple **20**
Phonetic symbols **36**
Pieces of things **48**
Plays (theatre) **19**
Politeness **30**
Present Perfect **20**
Present Perfect Continous **20, 25**
Present Simple **5, 20**
Pronunciation **10, 31, 36, 37, 49**
Proverbs **3, 43**
Punctuation **41, 49**
Quantity expressions **3, 24**
Riddles **12, 45**
Science fiction films **7**
Shapes **2**
Signs and notices **1, 6, 22, 50**
Songs **5, 20, 24, 43, 49**
Special days **39**
Spelling **7, 10, 32, 47**
Sports scores **33**
Telegram language **17**
Telephone expressions **38**
Time conjunctions **29**
*too much/too many*, etc. **24**
Verbs
– *be* + adverbial particles **35**
– contractions **49**
– *-ed* ending **20**
– ellipsis **4, 17**
– imperative/infinitive **5**
– in conditional sentences **18, 43**
– *-ing* ending **20, 49**
– passive **50**
– past participles **6, 50**
– Past Simple/Present Perfect **20**
– Present Perfect Continuous **20, 25**
– Present Simple **5, 20**
– the same as nouns **5**
Warning signs **1, 22, 50**